Hitler's Munich Man

'To-day, a "Man of Munich" is used by our gutter Press as a term of contumely. I wonder what our descendants a hundred years hence will have to say about it. Whatever their verdict, which largely depends on the nature of the "historians," I only desire that my name be written humbly on the scroll of the "Men of Munich"'

Sir Barry Edward Domvile 1943

Hitler's Munich Man
The Downfall of Admiral Sir Barry Domvile

Martin Connolly

Pen & Sword
MILITARY

First published in Great Britain in 2017 by
Pen & Sword Military
an imprint of
Pen & Sword Books Ltd
47 Church Street
Barnsley
South Yorkshire
S70 2AS

Copyright © Martin Connolly 2017

ISBN 978 1 52670 707 9

The right of Martin Connolly to be identified as the Author of this Work has been asserted by him in accordance with the Copyright, Designs and Patents Act 1988.

A CIP catalogue record for this book is
available from the British Library.

All rights reserved. No part of this book may be reproduced or transmitted in any form or by any means, electronic or mechanical including photocopying, recording or by any information storage and retrieval system, without permission from the Publisher in writing.

Printed and bound in England
by TJ International Ltd.

Pen & Sword Books Ltd incorporates the Imprints of Pen & Sword Books Archaeology, Atlas, Aviation, Battleground, Discovery, Family History, History, Maritime, Military, Naval, Politics, Railways, Select, Transport, True Crime, Fiction, Frontline Books, Leo Cooper, Praetorian Press, Seaforth Publishing, Wharncliffe and White Owl.

For a complete list of Pen & Sword titles please contact
PEN & SWORD BOOKS LIMITED
47 Church Street, Barnsley, South Yorkshire, S70 2AS, England
E-mail: enquiries@pen-and-sword.co.uk
Website: www.pen-and-sword.co.uk

Dedicated to the memory of those who perished under Nazism and to the brave men who gave their lives to defeat them.

'Monsters exist, but they are too few in number to be truly dangerous. More dangerous are the common men, the functionaries ready to believe and to act without asking questions.'

Primo Levi, Holocaust Survivor

Contents

Acknowledgements		viii
Introduction		ix
Chapter 1	Germany and Europe before the Great War	1
Chapter 2	Germany, Hitler and the British Pre-1940	6
Chapter 3	Admiral Sir Barry Edward Domvile	23
Chapter 4	Regulation 18B of the Defence (General) Regulations 1939	26
Chapter 5	A Man Is Known by the Company He Keeps	29
Chapter 6	The Reasons for the Domviles' Detention	40
Chapter 7	Domvile's Activity and MI5's Records	44
Chapter 8	The Cabin Boy's New Berth	60
Chapter 9	The Admiral's View of Himself	63
Chapter 10	The First Appearance before the Committee	71
Chapter 11	The Security Service Response to Domvile's Hearing	82
Chapter 12	Domvile Re-examined	92
Chapter 13	Further Hearings for Domvile	102
Chapter 14	Admiral Domvile after His Release	112
Chapter 15	What Domvile's Diaries Reveal	117
Chapter 16	Domvile in *Action*, *Patriot* and Other Writings	128
Conclusion		136
Bibliography and Sources		150
Index		152

Acknowledgements

No one ever truly writes in isolation. Around every writer there are resources and people who help towards the finished work. I am therefore grateful firstly to my wife Kitty who tolerates my many hours researching and writing and to my children for their support and encouragement.

I am also highly appreciative of those at Pen & Sword who have always been courteous and helpful with me as an author moving my idea from its conception through to the published work, especially the ever present Heather and her patience with my many questions.

There are also those resources I mentioned and I hope I have forgotten no one in the list that follows and if I have failed to acknowledge anyone, I will correct that in future editions.

To all of them I am as ever thankful.

Introduction

Whilst researching in the National Archives in London, my attention was drawn to a small passage that was not particularly within my then current research. However, because of my background in researching the Holocaust and the relationship between Jews and Christians, I was drawn to the description of a prominent Knight of the Realm and his anti-Semitic activities. As I pulled on this thread I unravelled the fascinating story of events from the Second World War that I had not been fully aware of. This book is the result of the discovery of that small passage.

The world has seen many wars. In them, dictators and national leaders have risen to impose their authority on others or to right a seeming injustice. The bloody battles of men using primitive bows and arrows, axes and knives in hand to hand combat gave way to gunpowder and the terror of death from a distance. At the beginning of the twentieth century, the world entered a decade of great uncertainty and change. In Europe, vast industrialisation saw the manufacture of new forms of weaponry and in the second decade of the century, war became a mechanised horror that would see tens of thousands killed or horrifically wounded within hours.

It was so momentous and involved many of the major countries, that it would be given the name the Great War. That war would be followed within twenty-five years by another horrific slaughter and the Great War would become the First World War (28 July 1914–11 November 1918) followed by the Second World War (1 September 1939–2 September 1945). Both these conflicts had Germany at their centre. Between these wars, pro-Germans and Fascists became a growing concern in Britain. This book does not attempt to give a complete analysis of fascism or pro-German activity in Britain. However, in order to appreciate the central point of this book, it is important to paint the backdrop to the rise of fascism, German sympathy and anti-Semitism in Britain between the wars.

What is sometimes lost in looking at history is that the grand sweep can cause important details to be missed. The early 1900s in England were a time of concern about Germany's military intentions after their campaigns in the late 1880s. The country was awash with rumours about what Germany was up to and the belief that their spies were living secretly throughout Britain. Newspapers were warning the population to be alert for 'foreign' strangers in their midst. The landed gentry were concerned about how imports were destroying the local economy, and their profits. Conservatism was feeling threatened by the issues being raised by Socialists and Communists. Protectionism was in the air and the conspiracy theory of international finance was at work. This in turn raised the supposed spectre of Jews being behind the scenes manipulating events.

Anti-Semitism had been a running thread through English history. It rose and fell with the tide of social upheaval when a scapegoat was needed to explain the problems behind the difficulties in the country. One man who typifies these attitudes was Houston Stewart Chamberlain who was a particular proponent of an idea that Hitler would later pick up. That was the belief that the Teutonic race was being polluted, especially by Jews. English-born, Chamberlain would move to Austria and marry Wagner's daughter Eva. Then there was Anthony Ludovici, who advocated that the only way to eradicate the influences of feeble Liberalism and Judaic/Christian ideas was through violence and physical extinction. Ludovici was born in England and in many ways leaned to Conservatism, but he believed in eugenics and the right of the hereditary aristocracy to rule. He would later become a member of the extreme Right Club and become an admirer of Hitler and his ant-Semitic policies. He was prolific in writing books and pamphlets on the matter.

The Boer war had ended and the British population was suffering from poverty. Workers were discontented and the seeds of the Labour Party were sown. The Women's Social and Political Union (WSPU), the Suffragettes, were agitating for reform of the democratic system. Britain had aligned with France, which led to Germany attempting to break that alliance. Chancellor David Lloyd George introduced his 'People's Budget' which was wrecked by the House of Lords. The Irish question and Home Rule was causing consternation. German gunboat activity in Moroccan waters, and the French/German pact that resulted, raised worries in Whitehall. The Liberals and Conservatives vied for government with Labour and Irish Nationalists making their own demands. War with Germany eventually came and with it the severe draconian measures of the Defence of the Realm Act and concerned liberal reactions. All this was the backdrop to a view that a strong hand was needed to protect the country. The seeds of a revival of anti-Semitism, Nationalism, and Dictatorship united in Fascism were sown and these would find flowering in the inter-war years.

When the First World War ended, Germany was in complete collapse. Britain emerged from the horrific campaign with a huge loss of young men and a grave economic crisis. The British government seemed powerless to stop the decline into a slump that would throw millions into unemployment. Trade Unionism had increased with a doubling of union membership to over eight million by 1920. On 8 May 1920, *The Times* printed an article anonymously *The Jewish Peril*, now known to have been the work of George Shanks who was born in Moscow of English parents. His family business was lost in the Russian revolution and he returned to London. For him, the Bolsheviks and Jews were responsible. *The Jewish Peril* was a translation of *The Protocols of the Elders of Zion*, which regurgitated the Jewish conspiracy theory. However, there were other voices such as that of the *Spectator* on 12 May 1920:

'In our opinion, the book is a piece of malignant lunacy. In the present condition of public opinion it is, however, likely to do an infinity of harm if it is allowed to go unchallenged, and if the better advisers of the public do not correct the maddening follies which can, and we fear may, be based upon an uninstructed study of this singular and most powerful though dangerous work.'

The *Protocols* have their origins in the French Revolution. A French Jesuit, Abbe Barruel, was opposed to the revolution and in 1797 he published a document blaming the trouble on a secret conspiracy by Freemasons. This would have been an odd claim as the French aristocracy was deeply Masonic, but he was probably influenced by an anti-Mason, Robinson, a Scottish mathematician. The Jews of France were emancipated by the Revolution and Barruel never blamed them in any way for it. In 1806, a forged letter surfaced in France alleging that the Jews and not Masons were behind the Revolution. This was at a time when Napoleon Bonaparte was formulating a policy of liberation for Jews. It was here where the false seeds of a secret conspiracy by Jews were formed. In 1864 the French satirist Maurice Joly, who was not a Jew, published *Dialogues in Hell between Machiavelli and Montesquieu*. This did not mention Jews but was a satirical attack on Napoleon III, for which Joly went to prison. Hermann Goedsche, a German anti-Semite who worked for the Prussian secret police, used a pseudonym, Sir John Retcliffe. Under this he forged a number of documents as evidence in a prosecution case. It was this man who took Joly's *Dialogues* and used them in 1868 as part of his series of novels entitled *Biarritz*. It was in a chapter in the novel that he wrote about 'The Council of representatives of The Twelve Tribes of Israel' and a secret rabbinical conference. From this fiction followed the conspiracy that became the *Protocols*. *The Times* newspaper over 16–18 August 1921 ran a full article detailing the history of the forgery. However, this mixture of anti-Semitism and Bolshevism was like rain on the seeds of fascism that was steadily growing in Britain.

January 1922 witnessed the emergence of an independent Free State in Ireland, threatening the stability of the British Empire. In India, March saw the imprisonment of Gandhi for pacifist agitation. That was bringing further alarm to the Empire. April in Russia saw the steel hand of Stalin take charge of the Russian Communist Party. October saw the emergence of Benito Mussolini as a dictator in Italy. Many in Britain admired him as he appeared to lift the poor out of their poverty and bring Italy into prosperity after the devastating war. With an eye to what had happened in Russia with the Tsar and a General Strike in 1926, the far Right in Britain felt increasingly threatened by what they saw as the Jewish/Bolshevik menace.

In Britain, there emerged among intellectuals a concern that governments brought about by democracy were failing to solve the needs of the country. Such men included the political scientist Claud Sutton, a member of the British Union of Fascists who was an apologist for fascism. He was a tutor at St Peter's Hall, Oxford. In his writings he was very clear:

> 'My belief is, that the present crisis is an ethical crisis rather than an economic crisis, and that it is in the main due to the unethical, ethos-destroying philosophy of 'general will' upon which the modern democratic state has been based; and also that this philosophy is dying. Put away your textbooks on the theory of General Will and on the intricacies of Representation; they will not be needed these fifty years!'

There was also Sir Charles Petrie. He was from Liverpool and graduated from Oxford to become an historian of some merit. He was a supporter of Fascism but he refused to support or accept Nazism. Initially he was a strong supporter of Oswald Mosley although he would in later years become much cooler in that support. He would later join the January Club. The January Club was a discussion group founded in 1934 by Oswald Mosley and others to attract Establishment support for the British Union of Fascists (BUF). Mosley was the founder of the BUF. He was the 6th Baronet of Ancoats in the county of Lancashire and after attending Winchester School, entered Sandhurst for officer training. They observed the strength of Mussolini as well as other strong national figures such as Horthy in Hungary, who had taken strong action to impose order in a crumbling country. He had banned the Communist Party and would later support Hitler in his ambitions against Russia. There was also Kemal Ataturk in Turkey, who had brought independence to his country and gave strong leadership to bring his nation into the twentieth century. A brave military man, he became the first President of modern Turkey, alongside others emerging in other parts of Europe and the BUF were inspired to develop Fascism further.

Initially, the flavour of Fascism in Britain was Italian. This was seen in the establishment of British Fascists (BF) who, whilst holding to mainstream Fascist ideals, did not initially lean to pro-German views or overt anti-Semitism. They were a broad mixture of traditional Conservatives and others who sought what they considered to be a better form of government. A main idea which a number of their followers embraced was Corporatism, defined by a Papal Commission in 1881 as a 'system of social organization that has at its base the grouping of men according to the community of their natural interests and social functions, and as true and proper organs of the state they direct and coordinate labour and capital in matters of common interest'.

In Britain, disputes within BF appeared with men like Arthur Leese, a virulent Fascist and anti-Semite. An army veterinary surgeon, he became convinced that the *Protocols of the Elders of Zion* were true. This led him to extreme activity in England to stir up anti-Jewish feelings. Originally a BF member, he decided they were too Tory for him and he joined the BUF, becoming a member under Mosley. He then decided that their policies and activities were too tame and accused the BUF of being 'kosher fascists'. He became influenced by another extreme anti-Semite, Henry Hamilton Beamish, and formed the Italian Fascist League (IFL). He also became enamoured with the Nazi idea of Aryanism and took a racial stance that would lead him in the 1930s to call for the extermination of Jews in the gas chamber. This brought him into conflict with the law and he was imprisoned for the extreme pamphlets and articles he was writing which were deemed to be causing public mischief. In his 'manifesto' he included Corporatism in which he called for a government that had an Upper House appointed by the State. The Lower House would consist of figures from industry and representatives from the Guilds of workers. In his plans, Jews would be denied citizenship. His idea of Government would not be a democracy, as was outlined in his editorial in the IFL's *The Fascist* magazine entitled, *Making Britain Safe from Democracy*.

On the scene were also the National Workers' Party. It was violently pro-Nazi and anti-Semitic. Its founder was Lt. Col. Graham Seton Hutchinson, a friend of Hitler, and he was in the pay of the Germans to promote them in Britain. Hutchinson played on the emotions of ex-servicemen and the unemployed and presented their situation as the responsibility of Jewish international influences.

Oswald Mosley had come from the ranks of traditional Conservatives. Unhappy with many of their policies, he sought to create an influence within the party that would change their direction. In the beginning, he kept his pro-German and anti-Semitism under control and gave the impression he leaned towards the Italian stream of Fascism. Indeed, Guy Liddell, of the Security Service, in his diary entry for 9 August 1945, writes of a letter he has seen from Mussolini that stated he was sending £60,000 a year to Mosley.

Eventually, Mosley would become frustrated with his lack of effect on traditional Conservatives and after disputes, established the BUF. Later he would add 'and National Socialists' to the name as he became more pro-German. As middle-class Tories deserted him he appealed to the working class by highlighting the evils of Jewish immigration as he saw it. Where such communities of immigrants existed, such as the East End of London, or the cotton manufacturing areas of North England, he and his speakers played on the fears of the unemployed and low paid workers - violence was never far away from their meetings.

He was in conflict with other fascist groups which he tried to assimilate into his BUF but they resisted. They all felt the same about Mosley and saw him only interested in his own advancement and not that of the workers of the country. However, the main groups mentioned above would eventually fade away and Mosley became the dominant voice of Fascism in Britain. The Fascists would enter the late 'thirties with a clear anti-Semitic attitude and pro-German with a liking for the Nazi systems, especially their colourful staging of events and uniforms. Mosley believed this would be attractive to the workers he sought to recruit. He also argued he was for Britain and the British Empire, which he saw threatened by the international conspiracy of the Jews. Whilst the majority of Mosley's followers, his foot soldiers, did come from the working class, he attracted some from the middle-class and upper ranks of society. Mosley was extremely active in attempts to prevent a war with Germany, blaming the Jews for provoking it and thus justifying Germany's treatment of them. By 1939, Mosley's fascism had brought together Nazism and anti-Semitism but he had been rejected by the majority of the Establishment and the British public. However, even within the Royal House of Windsor, echoes of Mosley's views could be found. In July 1933, the Prince of Wales said, 'It is no business of ours to interfere in German internal affairs either re Jews or re anything else.'

From the earliest days of Fascism in Britain one document in particular was an essential part of the basis of all fascists' beliefs about Jews. These were the *Protocols* mentioned earlier.

In that first Great War a naval officer rose to great heights in the service of Britain and its Empire. He fought against the Germans and played an important part in that country's defeat. Having served his country and been awarded all the honours of state, this officer retired as an Admiral and looked set for a well-earned peaceful retirement. With a passion for the British Empire he looked for ways to use his reputation to strengthen it and to see it flourish. Part of this desire led him to look to the defeated enemy, Germany, and to build relationships with that country, which he believed would yield peace in Europe and allow Britain to concentrate on the Empire. In seeking to build these relationships the naval hero took a path that brought him into contact with the Nazi leaders of Germany. These German leaders would eventually confront Britain and wage war against her. He also joined fellow travellers who held strong Fascist views and were strident anti-Semites.

Many of these also were sympathetic to Germany and the Nazi regime. A great deal of their activities was actively against British interests and it would suggest he too was betraying his country. The British Security Service (SIS) took an interest in his activities which led to him being arrested and incarcerated in Brixton prison, without trial, for being a danger to Britain. A photograph appeared in many newspapers on the day after his arrest. It showed the Admiral and his wife with a photograph of Hitler and a Stormtrooper statuette on their sideboard. The common consensus was that he was a Nazi sympathiser.

What was the truth about these allegations made against him? Was he pro-German and a supporter of the Nazi government? Did he conspire to bring about a fascist revolution in Britain? With the help of secret files and newspaper reports, what follows explores how this high ranking naval officer, Admiral Sir Barry Domvile, found himself in a cramped prison cell as an enemy of the country that he had served.

Chapter 1

Germany and Europe before the Great War

There are two versions of the start of the First German Reich (Empire). For some it was the crowning of Charlemagne in the year 800. Others point to the crowning of Otto I (Otto the Great) in the year 962. Whichever view is taken, it was the Peace of Westphalia at the end of the Thirty Years' War in 1648 that brought the effective end to this first German empire. It was finally confirmed in 1806 when Emperor Francis II abdicated following defeat by the French in 1805 when Napoleon sent his Grand Army into Germany. The mighty alliance of Russia, Britain, Austria, Netherlands, Sweden, Naples and the German states could not prevent his victory. The French procession through the Germanic territories saw the Tricolour waving over the soil of Austria and Germany. 27,000 Austrian soldiers survived and suffered the humiliation of laying down their arms to the victorious forces of Napoleon. The indigenous people rose up and they conducted widespread resistance to the French. Alongside their physical resistance, the people conducted a propaganda war. Pamphlets were issued condemning the French and calling for resistance to continue against them. Johannes Philipp Palm was a simple bookseller in Nuremberg who would not bend the knee and actively distributed the pamphlets. One such pamphlet entitled *Germany's Deepest Humiliation* was found in his possession. Arrested and interrogated, he refused to name the printer or publisher of the pamphlet. The French tried him in what was considered a mock trial and made an example of him. By Napoleon's orders, he was taken to Braunau-on-the-Inn and on 26 August 1806 he stood blindfolded before a French firing squad. The bullets of the French tore into his chest and he collapsed in a bloody heap. The seeds of resentment against anyone attempting to ever again destroy the future Germany were sown in the minds of its people by this history. Following Napoleon's defeat Prussia, Austria and France had intermittent conflicts. Mini revolutions arose within the various German states and they were not yet a truly united country. In Braunau-on-the-Inn in 1866, long after the French were finally expelled from Germany and Austria, a monument was erected to Johannes Philipp Palm.

In 1871 the German Empire (Second Reich) under Wilhelm I unified the states except for Austria, who as a great power in her own right, cherished her independence. Otto Von Bismarck emerged as the first Chancellor of Germany. Eventually the country regained its independence from outside forces and expanded its territories absorbing neighbouring colonies.

On 20 April 1889, Klara the wife of Alois Hitler gave birth to a son, Adolf. As the young boy grew, he was a withdrawn child and wandered alone through Braunau-on-the-Inn. At his school, he would learn of this humiliation of Germany and of the resistance of men like Palm. Often he came to the memorial of Johannes Philipp Palm and the stories of how Germany suffered under the French burned into his soul. He would write about this episode in later life and it would be an inspiration for his ambitions in Europe. He, like most Germans, had a resolve that Germany would never again be subjected to any foreign power. Never again would Germany be humiliated. Adolph Hitler would be called to put his life on the line to demonstrate that resolve.

Germany and Austria formed an alliance based on their historic relationships and a concern that France threatened their respective countries. Italy joined this alliance concerned that France would intervene in its attempt to increase territory in North Africa. France in turn sought to protect herself by throwing her lot in with Britain and Russia. This was further complicated by the Italians who secretly came to an agreement with France over the status of the Balkan territories. Italy and Spain meanwhile remained under the rule of their respective royal families, though not without their own internal troubles.

It has to be borne in mind that all parties in these alliances were prepared to abandon them if their own national interests were threatened and secret arrangements were frequently made with other parties. Thus the peace in Europe was always fragile because of these alliances and competing claims to territories and their boundaries. Quite unexpectedly, whilst Archduke Franz Ferdinand, heir to the throne of Austria-Hungary, was visiting Sarajevo, he was assassinated by a young Yugoslavian nationalist. This allowed the Austro-Hungarian Empire an opportunity to prevent the expansionist aims of Serbia in the Balkans by making impossible demands of the Serbians. These demands were not met and within a month, Europe was plunged into the darkness of war. Germany would invade Belgium and its old enemy France. Britain would make demands that were ignored and the result was the horrific Great War. It saw thirty-seven million casualties resulting in almost nine million deaths. Britain and her allies lost five million with Germany losing just fewer than three and a half million. Europe lay devastated in the wake of the war, with Germany brought to her knees.

Admiral Sir Barry Domvile commanded ships of Her Majesty's navy that were crucial in defeating Germany. The victorious allies imposed severe penalties on Germany, as the aggressor. These penalties were enshrined in the Treaty of Versailles on 28 June 1919. As a rising star in the Navy and being groomed for higher things in Naval Intelligence, Domvile was involved on the side-lines of the discussions on the treaty. He did not agree with the conclusions reached:

> 'The merit of a treaty of peace does not lie so much in the actual test of the conditions to be observed, as in the wisdom and foresight exercised in respect to the durable nature of the treaty. To some this may appear a distinction without a difference, but it is not so. For example, if the peace conditions are harsh, it is obviously necessary to arrange that they can be enforced and maintained without danger of retaliation, involving a further breach of the peace. To make a peace treaty which can neither be expected to endure, nor yet to be capable of enforcement, even after a further recourse to arms, is just silly.'

In Britain the response to the war was great anger against Germany. The slogans of the day reflect the hatred of the majority of the population. 'Hang the Kaiser' and 'Make Germany Pay' were the common cries in the newspapers. A typical example of the mood was reflected in the *Daily Record* on Tuesday 3 December 1918:

> HANG THE KAISER
> 'With a section of the most sober-thinking public calling for the death of the ex-Kaiser political candidates are finding it awkward to avoid any reference to the proposition. The heading I have given to this paragraph has become the popular catch phrase.'

From the Houses of Parliament to the bar at the local pub, the sentiment felt, as the soldiers and sailors returned home, was a determination that Germany must pay heavily for her actions. France particularly was vociferous in calling for the damages against Germany to be severe. Lloyd George presented a public face in support of these views but privately he had concerns. He was looking to Russia and feared the expansion of Communist influence throughout Europe. His thoughts were that Germany, if treated properly, would be a bulwark against any advance from Russia. Meanwhile, Woodrow Wilson, the American President, had such repugnance for the war that he wanted to separate himself from the problems of Europe and could not wait to get the whole matter out of his way. Italy had been treated with contempt by the Allies, even though it had fought on their side but without any great significance. They were excluded from the negotiations, because before the war they had been part of a tri-partite treaty with Germany and Austria. Italy had broken that treaty in 1915, by joining the side of the allies. Germany was therefore completely isolated, with few friends. The second German Reich came to an end in humiliation and defeat.

The penalties for Germany were severe. It lost a great amount of territory. France was given the Alsace-Lorraine area. Denmark was allowed to take Northern Schleswig. Poland received West Prussia, Posen and Upper Silesia. Hultschin was given to Czechoslovakia. Belgium took control of Eupen and Malmedy. The League of Nations took control of the Saar, Danzig and Memel with the intentions of allowing the populations to vote how they wished to be governed and by whom. All of these territories would become matters of great controversy in the run up to the Second World War. The League also took decisions to return to Russia land taken in the Treaty of Brest-Litovsk. The new states of Estonia, Lithuania and Latvia emerged. Poland expanded and received some of this land. This too would become an issue in the Second World War. Further humiliation of Germany came with restrictions on their military. Limited to 100,000 men in the army, they could not have tanks. Whilst they were permitted the use of gliders, there could be no proper air-force and only six naval ships were permitted. A demilitarised zone was imposed around the Rhine which no armed German could enter. France would later, against a background of protests from her allies, occupy the Ruhr region of Germany. Financially Germany stood on the precipice of bankruptcy. Furthermore, Germany would be forced to accept a 'war guilt' clause that held it responsible for starting the war and therefore responsible for making reparations to the allies for all damages to the countries on the allied side. There was no fixed amount for these. Germany had to accept signing a blank cheque which eventually would be £6.6 billion pounds. There was no conceivable way Germany would ever pay.

Germany had never been consulted on the Treaty. It was presented to them just weeks before they were due to sign it. They were given two options; sign or be occupied. They signed. The result was that throughout Germany, as the terms were made known, a great anger arose. The humiliation was too much for many. The Kaiser fled and a third German Reich was not considered amidst this disgrace. At Weimar, the idea of a republic was born and the Weimar Republic came into existence in the fervent hope of a democratic peaceful future for Germany; Berlin was not chosen for this momentous event because it was in turmoil as a Communist revolt was attempting to impose a Marxist state on Germany. These events would bring Adolph Hitler onto the world stage. He too, like Domvile, would come to disagree with the terms of the treaty.

Chapter 2

Germany, Hitler and the British Pre-1940

The simmering resentment of the German people, gave opportunity for Adolf Hitler, the ex-soldier, to come from obscurity. In the Great War, he had risen from private to corporal and showed great courage as a message runner for the German army. His actions brought him into danger and in time he was caught up in a gas attack that left him blind. There has been a debate about his blindness as to whether it was physical or psychosomatic. The evidence is not conclusive. Others involved in the particular gas attack described it as one of mustard gas, which would have physical results. The British records suggest it was White Star, another gas used in the war which was less harmful. Dr. Edmund Forster, who treated Hitler after the gas attack, was a specialist in soldiers suffering from hysteria. He had successfully treated many German soldiers, who had no physical injuries, but who complained of disabilities. It is recorded that Forster had told fellow medical colleagues the details of his treatment of Hitler and its psychosomatic nature. One of these was Ernst Weiss, a surgeon and novelist, who in turn wrote a fictional book, *Eye Witness*, which was a thinly disguised account of Hitler's treatment for psychosomatic blindness. Forster himself was found dead, apparently committing suicide at his home in Germany. It has been suggested his death was at the hands of the Nazis who were afraid he would reveal the true nature of Hitler's blindness.

Whatever the truth about his blindness, Hitler was awarded two Iron Cross medals for his part in the war, the last being first class, an unusual award for a corporal. In light of Hitler's subsequent slaughter of Jews it is ironic that the recommendation for the medal came from Hugo Gutmann, a Jewish officer.

The army had given this young man a purpose. He had been a drifter and failed to obtain entry into higher education to fulfil his dreams of being an artist. Throughout his drifting he developed a great hatred for Jews and believed them to be at the root of Germany's problems. After the war, his return to Germany was very traumatic. Released from the army, he no longer had any identity. The proud soldier saw Germany now a defeated nation, internally torn apart by divisions and externally, in his opinion, oppressed by the victorious allies, especially the French. He became convinced that Communism, and behind this, Jews, were the real cause of Germany's woes. As an agent recruited to spy on meetings of dissidents, he became caught up in German politics through the German Worker's Party. He became a charismatic speaker and his first major speech was recalled by him in his book *Mein Kampf* (My Struggle):

> 'I spoke for thirty minutes, and what before I had simply felt within me, without in any way knowing it, was now proved by reality: I could speak! After thirty minutes the people in the small room were electrified and the enthusiasm was first expressed by the fact that my appeal to the self-sacrifice of those present led to the donation of three hundred marks.'

This was not just an egocentric view; others around him also recognised his charismatic style and passionate delivery. So it was that Adolf Hitler became the leader of a political movement that emerged; the National Socialist German Workers' Party, the *Nationalsozialistische Deutsche Arbeiterpartei* or NSDAP which gave them the name Nazi.

In November 1923, Hitler believed he could overthrow the German government and embarked on what became known as the Beer Hall Putsch. Hitler had agreed with Colonel von Seisser, the head of the Bavarian State Police, to go to Berlin and prepare for a 'March on Berlin'. When the Bavarian government had been removed and the Nazis had assumed power, their government would be transferred to Berlin. Hitler told him, 'Colonel, I will wait until your return, but act then and persuade the *Generalstaatskommissar* [Gustav von Kahr, general state commissioner] to act'. He did not wait for the Colonel's return and suspicious that Kahr was in fact going to act against him, went ahead with his own plans. Unknown to him, Seisser had already conspired with Kahr to exclude Hitler from power.

The Putsch failed and he was tried and found guilty of treason. He was given a very lenient sentence, by sympathetic judges, to luxury imprisonment in Landsberg Prison in 1924 and it was there he wrote *Mein Kampf*.

This was to be his *Weltanschhauung*, his world view, which gave a terrifying warning to the world. The book became available in England in October 1933, even being serialised in *The Times* newspaper. It is certain that anyone in England who was pro-German would have been well aware of the book's content and Hitler's intentions.

It is important to look at these intentions and Hitler's world view when we consider how Germany under Hitler affected the situation in England, following the Great War.

The first thing that emerges from the opening chapters of *Mein Kampf* clearly shows that Hitler believed that democracy had failed and that the failure was due to the influence of the Jews, similar to the Fascist movements across the world. He believed in the inferiority of the other nations around Germany and of the need to rescue the true Germans from these countries. This became a focus for Hitler and was to be first realised in his intentions towards Austria:

> 'Because my heart was always with the German Empire and not with the Austrian Monarchy, the hour of Austria's dissolution as a State appeared to me only as the first step towards the emancipation of the German nation.'

It was clear that Hitler was never going to be content within the then current boundaries of Germany. For him, the rise of a Third Reich was the only solution. A Third Reich that would not make the mistakes of the past, but would impose an iron fist on its enemies.

Furthermore Hitler had become convinced that Darwinian Theory, which argued that in natural evolution the weakest of the animal species, would eventually die out and the stronger of the species would survive and develop, should be forcibly applied to humans. This would have been anathema to Darwin. Combining this with the theory of Eugenics, which believed in the creation of a unique pure man, a Master Race, he adopted a worldview that was seen in his intolerance of any human being he would see as weak or feeble, such people would not be tolerated:

> 'For as soon as the procreative faculty is thwarted and the number of births diminished, the natural struggle for existence which allows only healthy and strong individuals to survive is replaced by a sheer craze to

"save" feeble and even diseased creatures at any cost. And thus the seeds are sown for a human progeny which will become more and more miserable from one generation to another, as long as Nature's will is scorned.'

This view would be implemented by Hitler in the euthanasia programme against the mentally and physically handicapped that he believed should not be 'saved'.

Hitler did not disguise his intention that Germany would become violently aggressive. In his view the only nations that would survive would have to be by nature 'brutal':

'A time will come, even though in the distant future, when there can be only two alternatives: Either the world will be ruled according to our modern concept of democracy, and then every decision will be in favour of the numerically stronger races: or the world will be governed by the law of natural distribution of power, and then those nations will be victorious who are of more brutal will and are not the nations who have practised self-denial.'

Hitler was also clear about the policy of *Lebensraum* (living space). This was the expansion into neighbouring countries to facilitate the feeding and settlement of an increasing German population. The then current government had chosen a policy of commercial trade as the means of providing for its citizens. Hitler did not agree:

'Therefore the problem was: A policy of territorial expansion or a colonial and commercial policy. Both policies were taken into consideration, examined, recommended and rejected, from various standpoints, with the result that the second alternative was finally adopted. The sounder alternative, however, was undoubtedly the first.'

He went on to make clear that if the countries being taken over did not accept Germany's expansion into their lands, they would not be asked twice:

'And when attempts to settle the difficulty in an amicable way are rejected the clenched hand must take by force that which was refused to the open hand of friendship.'

Behind everything that Hitler thought was a disadvantage to Germany, he saw the problem as a Jewish-Marxist conspiracy. This was very true about those in Germany who may not have been fully supportive of a German victory in the Great War. Hitler would have preferred his government to 'exterminate this vermin' and when he became the government that is exactly what he did. The 'doctrine' of Jewish-Marxism that he railed against had to be defeated and his answers in *Mein Kampf* foreshadowed the systematic genocide that he undertook:

> 'When sheer force is used to combat the spread of a doctrine, then that force must be employed systematically and persistently.'

In *Mein Kampf* he indeed was specific as to his prime motive:

> 'For a fight it will have to be, since the first objective will not be to build up the idea of the People's State [Germany] but rather to wipe out the Jewish State [Jews wherever they exist] which is now in existence.'

Hitler's ambitions were made clear and he betrayed his megalomania further by believing that if he had been in charge during the Great War 'the outcome of the struggle might have been different'. He saw himself as a great thinker and mastermind of a race of perfect human beings. He advocated a policy of state control of some of the most basic intimate aspects of life, including sexual relations and reproduction. Anyone deemed to be 'defective' would not be allowed to produce children:

> 'The demand that it should be made impossible for defective people to continue to propagate defective offspring is a demand that is based on most reasonable grounds, and its proper fulfilment is the most humane task that mankind has to face.'

This foreshadowed his programme of 'Aryanisation' that he would introduce to try and create his master race. In *Mein Kampf* he outlined his notions of how he would achieve such a race. It would involve the separation of the races, as he saw it:

'… whenever Aryans have mingled their blood with that of an inferior race the result has been the downfall of the people who were the standard-bearers of a higher culture.'

From this warped thinking came *Gesetze zum Schutz des Deutschen Blutes und der Deutschen Ehre*. (the Nuremberg Laws for the Protection of German Blood and German Honour). At the root of this law was anti-Semitism. The belief that there was not one human race but a superior race (Aryans) and the inferior races, the chief of which, in Hitler's view, were the Jews. Hitler, like many anti-Semites, clung to the libels of the *Protocols*, despite their long proven forgery status, and in *Mein Kampf* uses them to help justify his views. His warped obsession with the master race led him to believe that any state (country) that did not support the existence and survival of the master race did not deserve to exist:

'Those States which do not serve this purpose have no justification for their existence.'

This pointed clearly to the real agenda for the future which would see Germany, under Hitler, try to achieve world domination. By 1941, there was a growing concern in the House of Commons as to the British Empire being under threat from Hitler. Churchill himself spoke in the House on May 7 1941:

'It must be remembered, however, that Napoleon's armies carried with them the fierce, liberating and equalitarian winds of the French Revolution, whereas Hitler's Empire has nothing behind it but racial self-assertion, espionage, pillage, corruption and the Prussian boot. Yet Napoleon's Empire, with all its faults, and all its glories, fell and flashed away like snow at Easter till nothing remained but His Majesty's ship "Bellerophon," which awaited its suppliant refugee. So I derive confidence that the will-power of the British nation, expressing itself through a stern, steadfast, unyielding House of Commons, once again will perform its liberating function and humbly exercise and execute a high purpose among men, and I say this with the more confidence because we are no longer a small Island lost in the Northern mists, but around us gather in proud array all the free nations of the British Empire.'

Hitler also addressed the issue of the Treaty of Versailles and was again clear:

'For these reasons also the National Socialist Movement has to take up a stand against such tendencies [Those who accepted the Treaty in Germany].'

Whilst a complete critique of *Mein Kampf* cannot be undertaken here, there is sufficient detail for the reader to understand that those who were pro-German in Britain should have had a clear understanding of where Hitler stood. However, it is notable that in Guy Liddell's diary the Security Service regretted not paying more attention to *Mein Kampf*.

In *Mein Kampf*, Hitler told us exactly what he was going to do, and did it. Nobody paid much attention until the war started.

In his rabble-rousing speeches, Hitler had whipped up passionate feelings against the perceived injustices of the Treaty. He took hold of the German people's feeling and gave them a focus for their anger. It was a Jewish – Communist plot that had ruined Germany, he argued, and through his persuasive oratory, he led the nation to embrace National Socialism. It is often forgotten that Hitler's rise to power was through the democratic process, no matter how we interpret that, in Germany at the time. The author remembers during a visit to Germany, seeing a poster from the 1930's elections where the Nazis had stunning success. The poster has the image of Hitler alongside the legend, '*Unsere größte Hoffnung*' - 'Our Greatest Hope'. For 36.8 per cent of the German electorate in 1932 this was true. On the morning of 30 January 1933, Adolf Hitler was sworn in as Chancellor by Hindenburg, the elected President of Germany. Writing shortly after that, William Arnold-Forster, who was sympathetic to this new Germany, had one major reservation and had warned, in his book on Germany's concentration camps, against the atrocities of the regime. Indeed a review of the literature and articles in the main British newspapers, The Times and The Observer, in particular, show that a number of men with integrity and who were well meaning, argued for an accommodation with Hitler, as the least of the evils of that time. All of them echoed Arnold-Forster's call for Germany to abandon the persecution of 'Christians, Jews and liberal pacifists' and for all visitors to Germany to make that clear to the Nazi leaders.

Furthermore, Hitler and his Government had been hard at work to create relationships with Britain through their foreign office and the offices of Joachim von Ribbentrop, Adolf Hitler's adviser on Foreign Affairs from 1938 onwards (He was later convicted as a war criminal at the Nuremberg Trials and sentenced to death). Attempts were made to get the Prime Minister Ramsay MacDonald to visit Hitler in Germany. However he was not keen and avoided the invitation. Ribbentrop also promoted trips by leading citizens and journalists to Germany. They often returned as the best propagandists for the Nazi regime. This even spread to school exchange visits where children would be given a rosy view of how National Socialism saved Germany and how Adolf Hitler was a great man who as a child defended children against bullies at his school. This was brought into life by a text book published for schools, '*Adolf Hitler – Der Führer des deutschen Reiches. - A short account of his life and works*' co-authored by a German master, H E Lewington at the John Ruskin School, Croydon.

Part of this activity to bring German propaganda to Britain was the invitation to the Nuremberg rallies by Ribbentrop of many leading military and establishment figures. A further very successful strategy was to involve ex-servicemen in his propaganda plans. He organised exchange visits between ex-servicemen of Germany and Britain. For the initial visit his agent in England even persuaded the Prince of Wales to endorse and announce it at a British Legion rally. The King would later rebuke the Prince for this, although he never regretted it. Ribbentrop, Hess and Goering would speak to the ex-service men in Germany and paint a picture of noble enemies who had once fought but who both were now enemies of the Russian Bolsheviks. As they were both enemies of Russia that meant they were now friends. On visits to Germany the ex-servicemen were lavished with hospitality and came back with great impressions of Germany and Hitler. At least at a leadership level this was true but many of the ordinary ex-servicemen were not so convinced. Yet it did add to the overall favourable view of Germany and encouraged the establishment of Anglo/German links such as The Anglo German Fellowship (AGF) and its counterpart in Germany, the '*Deutsch Englische Gelleschaft*'. Ribbentrop also courted the airmen of Britain who had fought so well in the First World War. He exploited the genuine respect and honour both sides had for one another. Men like Lord Mottistone, a great friend of Ribbentrop, who was a strong apologist for Germany and Lord Sempill who would later join Admiral Domvile in a pro-Nazi organisation. Then there was the Secretary of State for Britain's air force, Lord Londonderry, who visited Germany to meet Ribbentrop, Goering and Hitler. He returned and became an extremely sympathetic supporter of the Nazi regime. His sympathies for the Nazi government earned him the nickname, 'Londonderry Herr'. However this seemed to waver after Germany invaded Prague. He would become active in Anglo German friendship groups. Another prominent figure was T P Conwell-Evans who started out as supporters of Hitler's rise and establishment of a Nazi state. Conwell-Evans was active in promoting Germany in Britain. Later he would become cooler in his support for the regime. He too would become associated with Admiral Domvile. Conwell-Evans accompanied Lloyd George who eventually went to meet Hitler at the *Berghof*, his alpine retreat. The meeting included Joachim von Ribbentrop and his wife Annelies, Megan Lloyd George, Gwilym Lloyd George, Thomas Jones, Lord Dawson of Penn, General Baron Geyr von Schneppenburg (Military Attaché in London), Otto Meissner (Head of the Presidential Chancellery), Dr Schmidt (as interpreter) and A J Sylvester who recorded the event on film. After this Lloyd George increasingly became an admirer of Hitler:

> 'I have now seen the famous German leader and also something of the great change he has effected. Whatever one may think of his methods - and they are certainly not those of a Parliamentary country - there can be no doubt that he has achieved a marvellous transformation in the spirit of the people, in their attitude towards each other, and in their social and economic outlook. One man has accomplished this miracle. He is a born leader of men. A magnetic dynamic personality with a single-minded purpose, a resolute will, and a dauntless heart.'

Lloyd George later opposed any appeasement of Hitler. However, this might have been more to do with his dislike of Neville Chamberlain because after the Battle of Britain Lloyd George wanted a negotiated peace with Germany.

The German charm offensive with people like Lloyd George continued, even though the signs of Nazi intolerance and ill-treatment of Jews was well known. Furthermore, evidence of a breach of the Versailles Treaty in building up his military was overlooked and Hitler and Ribbentrop were quite successful in developing a pro-German sympathy within Britain. This allowed Hitler to progress his plans and he would eventually declare the Treaty null and void and demanded the right to take back 'their' territory that had been given away by the allies.

Hitler's first step towards this was his re-occupation of the Rhineland on 7 March 1936. This was pivotal for increased pro-German support in Britain and displayed a brilliant strategic move by Germany to this end. In 1935 France had agreed a pact with Russia. This Franco/Russian pact caused alarm in Britain, with Communists being the great bogeymen. Britain had an agreement with France that she would come to France's aid if she were attacked. However, it was clear that politicians and the people of Britain did not want that to go any further. The pact with Russia increased anti-French feeling. This was exacerbated by France's support for Italy in Abyssinia when Italy invaded that country on 3 October 1935. Britain opposed Italy as the aggressor. The French support was in the hope that Italy would aid France against any German aggression. Further complication in the relationships Britain was trying to maintain, with France, Italy and Germany came in December 1935 with the Hoare/Laval pact. This would have given Italy a large proportion of Abyssinia as an Italian colony. Uproar in Britain from both right and left as well as from France caused it to be abandoned.

Ribbentrop was busy in the background in Britain, with a flow of very well placed people flocking to meet him in London. He was whispering in their ears that France was courting communism and Britain should be aware. The Franco/Russian pact was officially signed and ratified in February 1936 and Hitler used this as the excuse for the March occupation of the Rhineland. In Britain the growing anti-French feeling combined with a widespread view that Germany was only moving into her own territory, denied to her by the Versailles Treaty, which by now was in ruins anyway and was thought unfair by many. Further feelings against France increased as elections there in April and May 1936 brought the Popular Front to power. 5,628,321 people had voted for Communists, Radicals and Socialists. The great fear of Communism was again raised in Britain. Ribbentrop was continuing to stoke up this concern and tried to drive a wedge between Britain and France.

Hitler was doing his part to create division by calling for friendship between France and Germany, inviting France to walk into his trap, which they did. Their insistence that Germany should join the League of Nations was a matter they thought Germany would never do. Hitler then made his peace proposals towards France, which indeed included a willingness to join the League. France's belligerent response succeeded in bringing a substantial number in Britain to become pro-German. Admiral Domvile was one of those people. Combined with this there was a deliberate 'quieting' of extreme activity in Germany as they prepared for the Olympics to be held in Berlin. The Fascists groups were jubilant and encouraged pro-German feelings. The BUF's paper, Action was now publishing article after article proclaiming Germany as the country of peace. Pro-Nazism was now promoted by Mosley.

Ribbentrop was still busy trying to woo Britain. He worked assiduously for a meeting between Hitler and Prime Minister Baldwin. He had very little success as both Baldwin and Anthony Eden the Foreign Secretary were concerned about Germany's true intentions and their own concerns for France. However a good number of Lords and Ladies went to the Olympics in Berlin as Hitler's personal guests and all returned to Britain more enamoured than ever by Hitler's charm and Ribbentrop's manipulations. How far Hitler had fooled Lloyd George is seen in a statement Lloyd George made in the Daily Express in Sept 1936, 'The German's have definitely made up their minds never to quarrel with us again'.

Ribbentrop used the Nuremberg Rally of 1936 to invite a great number of British pro-Germans and those who were lukewarm. They would include Admiral Domvile. They were lavishly treated and installed in luxury accommodation and driven everywhere by a Storm-trooper chauffeur. Despite all this Ribbentrop knew he had not won the Foreign Office and realised that he would have grave problems in winning over the Government because of the British diplomats. He knew he needed to win over prominent establishment figures to persuade them. As he headed to Britain to take up the role of Ambassador in a pro-German atmosphere, this was his challenge. To assist him he sent ahead a delegation of German ex-servicemen led by Queen Victoria's grandson the Duke of Sax Coburg and Gotha, an extreme Nazi supporter. This manipulation of an honourable British Legion was typical of his strategies.

In understanding the pro-German forces in Britain, we also have to consider other events surrounding 1936. Hitler had made accord with Austria, in many minds, strengthening his peace credentials. In Spain the rise of Republicanism and Communist influence was concerning the British Government. The revolt of the Nationalists in Spain caused a dilemma in Britain. To support the Republican side would be seen as a support of Communism. To support the Nationalists would be to support a fascist regime. Germany and Italy declared support and sent resources to the Nationalists whilst Russia sent resources to the Republicans. France was concerned at a Nationalist victory as it would mean they faced a trio of fascist forces around them. Britain decided on very strong neutrality on the issue and banned military supplies. It even made it a criminal offence for British citizens to join the conflict. Over 4000 defied that step and went to Spain to fight. People in Britain held different views but in the main there was little shift in anti-French attitudes nor in pro-German support. The British fascists of course were vocal in support of the Nationalists, hoping for a fascist Government to join Italy and Germany in the international pantheon, which they sincerely hoped Britain would one day join. Indeed the publications from the pro-German side of the argument were calling for an alliance between Germany, Italy and Britain against the Bolshevik threat of Russia.

Britain entered a crisis towards the end of 1936 when Edward VIII abdicated. As Prince of Wales he had, as we have seen, appeared to be pro-German and favourable towards Hitler. Ribbentrop had hoped that as pro-German feeling increased, the Prince, now King may work favourably for alliance between Germany and Britain. Indeed, in his memoirs Ribbentrop bemoaned the abdication as a lost opportunity for the Anglo/German cause. Guy Liddell notes in his diary for August 24 1945, that microfilm recovered from the German Foreign offices, after the war, confirm Ribbentrop had also suggested that the Duke was not averse to being restored to the throne, believing that if he were still king, the war would never have happened. The secret files that Liddell said were recovered also show that Charles Bedaux, who advised the Duke, was involved in the matter.

Anti-Semitism in Germany had now been sent to the back of the minds of the British people. Germany's treatment of the Church in Germany and the arrests of over 700 Protestant pastors and the establishment of a state-controlled Church, did not seem to affect the attitudes of Britain in any substantial way. Reports in Britain of talk within Germany of its intentions to re-take the former German Colonies and a reported speech by Hitler in January 1937 caused no real waves of concern among the British people. It seemed that Germany had succeeded in lulling public opinion into an acceptance that German affairs were a matter for Germany. This is not to say there were no voices of dissent raised, but in general these did not seem to have any great influence and were confined to churchmen. 1937 saw the tension of this pro-German feeling and that of a sense of threat by a more strident and growing Germany. The announcement by the self-exiled Duke of Windsor and his new wife that he would be visiting Germany, caused consternation in the Foreign Office and Secret Service. Although he had stated that the visit was one of social concern, he cannot have been so naïve as not to realise the significance of an ex-king of Britain visiting Germany, during a time of high anxiety in Europe. The images of him meeting Nazi leaders, Hitler, Goering, Hess, Goebbels and Himmler and reviewing Nazi Storm Troops would make chilling viewing. However, the coverage in Britain was not given the greatest prominence and whilst there was some strong reaction in some quarters, in general the matter soon passed. However, as usual the fascist pro-German population welcomed the visit as 'an endorsement' of their support for Germany and the Nazi regime. In hindsight, the visit may have been a mixture of the Duke wanting to exercise his freedom of political thought, just as he had done in his marriage. It is also true he was given bad advice from those around him, especially Charles Bedaux, his host in Austria. Bedaux was a Frenchman who made every effort to befriend British Royalty and prominent Nazis. He had taken American citizenship in 1906 and his business enterprises made him a millionaire. He actively worked for the Nazis in France and abroad. The Duke of Windsor was married at his home in Paris and he arranged their honeymoon in Germany, where they met Hitler.

The elevation of Neville Chamberlain to Prime Minister in 1937 was preceded by the dispatch to Berlin of Sir Nevile Henderson as ambassador to Germany. Henderson was seen as sympathetic to Germany and as an appeaser of Hitler. This is reflected in his cable in February 1939, 'If we handle him [Hitler] right, my belief is that he will become gradually more pacific. But if we treat him as a pariah or mad dog we shall turn him finally and irrevocably into one.' A speech Henderson gave to the *Deutsch-Englische Gesellschaft* in

Berlin was designed by him to provoke a response in Britain. In it he praised Germany and described 'German philosophy and ideals' as the 'noblest in the world'. He stated that both Germany and Britain misunderstood each other but that there should be 'goodwill and peaceful cooperation' between them. Back home, there was outrage by some and congratulations by others in response to the speech. The Foreign Office did not accept the tone of the speech as it trod the difficult path between German, Italian and French relationships. Chamberlain himself was more inclined to Henderson's line as he had already told him to seek cooperation with Germany. Cabinet papers show Chamberlain argued for this with his Cabinet and in dealing with the Italian problem it was best to 'cultivate better relations with Germany'. There is no doubt that in defiance of the Versailles Treaty, the German navy was expanded and an air-force developed. There was a growing mood of concern in Britain and because of a reluctant official stance to make friendly alliances with Germany and she grew more distant in the Anglo/German relationship.

In March of 1938, Hitler's troops entered Austria and brought it into the *Anschluss*, the Nazi propaganda term for the invasion and forced incorporation of Austria to Nazi Germany, breaking the Versailles Treaty and without any interference from the allies. Opinion in Britain was divided and a dilemma posed for pro-Germans. The more extreme Fascists such as Lord Redesdale declared that the whole world owed Germany a 'debt of gratitude' for their action in Austria. Concern about another European war was growing. The rising tensions about Czechoslovakia and its German speaking population filled the British press. The threat of a German invasion was real, as was the clamour for Britain to stay out of it. Chamberlain brought Britain, France and Italy into an agreement to seek a resolution with Hitler which resulted in the Munich Agreement in September 1938. This laid Czechoslovakia, against her will, on the altar as a sacrifice for no war in Europe. Many politicians in Britain opposed the appeasement believing, rightly as it transpired, Hitler could not be trusted. The pro-Germans and Fascists, who remained solidly behind Germany, were certain that appeasement was the correct path. After the war, the truth would emerge that Hitler had been planning war on Czechoslovakia even as he talked with Chamberlain.

Chamberlain returned to England assuring the nation that there would be 'peace for our time', convinced that there would be no war and that Hitler would not make any further moves into other territory. He would be disappointed – further expansion into Czechoslovakia ensued. Germany also began to demonstrate that its anti-Jewish policy had not gone away.

Reinhard Heydrich, second-in-command of the SS, expelled about 17,000 Jews of Polish origin, including over 2,000 children, on October 27 1938. This would have most tragic repercussions. Among the Jews expelled were the Grynszpan family from Hanover. The son of this family was Herschel, an orthodox Jew. He had gone to live in Paris and was angered by the treatment of the Jews of Poland, including his own family. On 7 November, he purchased a gun and went to the German Embassy in Paris and shot the Secretary of Legation, Ernst von Rath.

Von Rath would die from his injuries on 9 November. Goebbels saw an opportunity to incite the German people to 'rise in bloody vengeance against the Jews'. From 9-10 November 1938, *Kristallnacht* showed the ugly face of Nazism using the excuse of the Paris death for the continued persecution of Jews. Jewish homes, hospitals, synagogues and schools were attacked and destroyed and over 100 Jews killed. That number excludes those who had 'disappeared' and were tortured and murdered in subsequent days. 25,000 Jewish men were taken and sent to Dachau, Buchenwald and Sachsenhausen concentration camps; many of them were tortured and killed by the SS.

The headlines in British newspapers carried the news of this terror against the Jews.

'GERMANY'S DAY OF WRECKING AND LOOTING
Gangs unhampered by the police
SYNAGOGUES BURNED DOWN IN MANY CITIES'
Manchester Guardian 11 November 1938

'THE ANTI-JEWISH OUTRAGES IN GERMANY
Whole Jewish Population Taken Away'
Manchester Guardian 12 November 1938

'Pogrom goes on till night
LOOTING MOBS DEFY GOEBBELS
Jewish homes fired, women beaten'
Daily Express 11 November 1938

This headline is interesting, as Goebbels did broadcast on German radio calling for the looting to stop, but this was a sham as he had personally given instructions to a gathering of SS units to carry out the pogrom. A *Times* reporter on 15 November summed up the situation, 'the condition of the Jews here is one of misery, terror and despair'. It appears that Lord Mount Temple's eyes were finally opened and he resigned from the AGF. What is perhaps telling is that only 20 out of the 900 AGF members joined his protest. The effect of this coverage was a hardening of opinion against Germany in the wider British population and either a turning of a blind eye or outright justification for the action by the far right in Britain.

Cola.Ernest Carroll was one such pro-Nazi to do so. He was an Australian who had served in the Great War. Although badly injured and left with some disability, he joined the Royal Flying Corp and was shot down and captured. Escaping from captivity, he returned to London. In an article in the *Anglo-German Review*, (This was the newspaper of the Link founded in 1937 as an organisation designed to promote good relationships with Germany, that Domvile would co-found), Carroll compared the violence in Germany to an attack on the pro-Nazi Unity Mitford in Hyde Park, by a crowd who objected to her wearing a Nazi badge. She was the obsessed with Adolf Hitler writing after she had met him for the first time that 'she would now be happy to die'. Mitford was only slightly hurt and was sent home on a bus by the police. Carroll wrote, 'Must one be a German Jew to get sympathy today?' Domvile, for the Link, issued a statement which deplored 'the recent embitterment of the Jewish question in Germany ... we realise with grief the violent revulsion of feeling caused in this country'. The statement went on to encourage the continued friendship with Germany where 'a kindlier spirit' would prevail. No outright or direct condemnation was given and what is notable is that the Link membership increased following that period.

As 1939 moved on it was clear that British public opinion in the main was concerned about Germany and the possibility of war. The only real public enthusiasts left for Germany were the BUF and the Link. The extreme far right men like Ramsay and Mosley tried to resurrect the conspiracy theories based on the *Protocols*, but it was now becoming increasingly difficult to drum up support for Germany.

Many in Britain had been angered by Chamberlain's approach to Hitler, calling his actions appeasement. However, there were some, as we have seen, who wholeheartedly agreed with Chamberlain and wanted to be identified with him. A growing minority of the population embraced the ideas and beliefs of Hitler and turned them into their own versions of political thought. These were the Fascists who would seek to bring to England an undemocratic corporatist government. They hoped that such a government would impose many of the principles of Hitler, particularly his anti-Semitic ideas of a Jew-free and white population.

On 23 August 1939, Germany and Russia signed a non-aggression treaty. Germany was preparing for further aggression in another direction and on 1 September 1939 invaded Poland, breaking its promises to Britain and France. By 3 September, Hitler had ignored all warnings and Britain with France declared war on Germany. The world was at war.

Admiral Sir Barry Edward Domvile, passionate about the rightness of the Munich Agreement, was a disappointed man on the outbreak of war. Since the founding of the Link he had been accused of aligning with the enemies of his country and plotting a fascist revolution in Britain. The admiral continued to sail into a clash with the state and was shipwrecked on rocks of his own making. It is that voyage we now turn to.

Chapter 3

Admiral Sir Barry Edward Domvile

In 1878, at the Royal Navy College Greenwich, Admiral Sir Compton Domvile, GCB, became the proud father of a son and named him Barry Edward. The admiral had the sea in his blood and had served his country with distinction. The young Barry was to follow in his father's footsteps. On 15 July 1892, at fourteen years of age, he entered the Royal Naval College to join HMS Britannia. From 1894 to 1897 he served as a midshipman, under sail, and on the emerging steam ships of the Royal Navy. In 1898, the young midshipman had proved himself and was promoted to sub-lieutenant. It was by special promotion in the same year he rose to lieutenant. His success in the Navigation and Pilotage for the rank of lieutenant, earned him the Beaufort Testimonial, which was founded in 1880 to commemorate the service of Rear-Admiral Sir Francis Beaufort. K.C.B., who filled the post of Hydrographer of the Navy from 1829 to 1855, consists of a prize of instruments or books of a professional character and of practical use to a Naval Officer. It is bestowed annually on the Midshipman who passes the best examination in Navigation and Pilotage for the rank of Lieutenant in the Royal Navy.

He also took the Ryder Prize for his French examinations. The Ryder Memorial Fund-founded in memory of Admiral of the Fleet, Sir Alfred Phillipps Ryder, K.C.B., and was awarded to the Sub-Lieutenant who takes the first place at the examination in French at the Royal Naval College. The prize consists of a book or books selected by the recipient with the approval of the President, Royal Naval College, Greenwich.

There is no doubt this young man was proving an able member of the Royal Navy, despite what he would later suggest was a Masonic plot against him. In 1906, a further commendation of his efforts came in the form of the prestigious Gold Medal of the Royal United Service Institution. From 1910 to 1911, Domvile commanded destroyers. His career moved forward and with the threat of war, he was appointed the Secretary to the Committee of Imperial Defence.

When war did come, he commanded the ships, *Miranda*, *Tipperary*, *Lightfoot*, *Arethusa*, *Carysfort*, *Centaur* and *Curacao*, bravely serving his country. For part of that time he served as Flag Captain to Admiral Sir Reginald Tyrwhitt. It was in February 1916 that he married his cousin Alexandrine von de Heydt. Through her mother, Alexandrine was the great granddaughter of Sir Robert Peel. Barry's mother was also from the Peel line. Alexandrine was the daughter of a German Baron Daniel Von De Heydt, a banker and later a director of a German company. The Von De Heydt bank was liquidated by the British Government in 1917. At the time of the marriage, the SIS noted the union of an active high ranking officer in the Royal Navy and a woman, the daughter of a German, whose country was then at war with England. No action was taken. The marriage would produce three children, Barry, Compton and Miranda.

Also in 1917, Barry Domvile became a Companion of the Most Distinguished Order of St. Michael and St. George. After the war, he became the Assistant Director and later Director of the Plans Policy Division of the Admiralty Naval Staff. This led him to represent his country at many conferences which took him to Brussels, Spa, Paris, San Remo, and Washington. In 1922, he became the Chief of Staff to Sir Osmond Brock, with the Mediterranean Fleet. He also joined the venerable ranks of the Most Honourable Order of the Bath. From 1925 to 1926 he commanded the *Royal Sovereign*. From 1927 to 1930, he progressed to the rank of Rear-Admiral, holding the post of Director of Naval Intelligence. This post brought him into an important position of trust and gave him access to highly sensitive information. It would later become a matter of concern for the Admiralty. From 1930 to 1931, he took command of the Third Cruiser Squadron of the Mediterranean Fleet, rising to Vice-Admiral. He was President of the Royal Naval College from 1932 to 1934, also holding the post of Vice-Admiral Commanding the War College. In 1934, King George V made him a Knight Commander of the Most Excellent Order of the British Empire.

Domvile cut a dashing figure as a man of the sea. His career and his moving within the higher circles of society brought him into contact with many of the leading ladies of that set. It was rumoured that the Admiral was not averse to coming under the spell of some of them. Ever the gentleman, the Admiral was always discreet and his good lady wife, given the affectionate nickname, 'Pudd' by Domvile, ever tolerant. His retirement from the Royal Navy as Admiral came in 1936.

It was from those dizzy heights of service to his country that Sir Barry Edward Domvile KBE CB CMG fell. He was not alone in his humiliation. His wife and son Compton were also detained. In his book *From Admiral to Cabin Boy* he himself wrote:

> 'Only the downward slope is in view, and the pitch is so steep that it amounts almost to a fall, against which my family motto '*Qui stat caveat ne cadat*' ['let he who has status beware, lest he fall'] warned me.'

Domvile had high hopes that Chamberlain's trip to Munich would bring peace with Germany and that the policy of appeasement of Germany would continue. When he wrote in 1943 that he wanted to be counted among the men of Munich, he was doing so in response to those who had called them *Guilty Men*. A book with this title was published in 1940 under the pseudonym 'Cato' (This was in fact Frank Owen and Michael Foot, journalists at the Evening Standard along with Peter Howard of the Sunday Express). The book held the Munich men responsible for the war especially the devastating events of Dunkirk and an expected invasion by the Nazis. Domvile, now arrested, was now deemed to be a guilty man for his pro-German activity.

What happened to bring this man who had served his country to this state?

A fellow member of the far right and friend of Domvile, Francis Yeats-Brown, a retired soldier, a member of the January Club and the Right Club, a man who praised Franco and Hitler, wrote to *The Times*, 'Why, for instance was Sir Barry Domvile arrested? It is true he encouraged Anglo-German friendship before the war, but does that make the distinguished Admiral a traitor?' Yeats-Brown raised this question because he knew that Domvile was a supporter of Germany and a fellow supporter of fascist groups with which they were both associated. The government's action to begin to detain fascists raised alarm bells with them and as a military man he believed the best form of defence was attack.

The question he raised is the question we now explore.

Chapter 4

Regulation 18B of the Defence (General) Regulations 1939

The relevant section of the act that concerns Admiral Domvile was:

'If the Secretary of State has reasonable cause to believe any person to have been or to be a member of, or to have been or "to be active in the furtherance of the objects of, any such organisation as is hereinafter mentioned", and that it is necessary to exercise control over him, he may make an order against that person directing that he be detained. The organisations hereinbefore referred to are any organisation as respects which the Secretary of State is satisfied that either— (a) the organisation is subject to foreign influence or control, or (b) the persons in control of the organisation have or have had associations with persons concerned in the government of, or sympathies with the system of government of, any Power with which His Majesty is at war. and in either case that there is danger of the utilisation of the organisation for purposes prejudicial to the public safety, the defence of the realm, the maintenance of public order, the efficient "prosecution of any war in which His Majesty may be engaged or the maintenance of supplies or services essential to the life of the community".'

18B allowed the internment without trial of British nationals suspected of being Nazi sympathisers or a danger to the State. The Foreign Office gave the following categories:

1. People of hostile origin;
2. People of hostile associations;
3. People who had recently been concerned in acts prejudicial to the public safety or the defence of the realm;
4. People who had recently been engaged in the preparation of such acts;
5. People who had recently been engaged in the instigation of such acts.

The effect of 18B was to suspend the right of affected individuals to habeas corpus and to be confined without trial. The bringing in of these powers was not without controversy and in the House of Commons many objections were raised and concerns expressed about detainees' rights. The situation was compared to the building of the Nazi concentration camps, such as Dachau, Germany, that were beginning to be established.

By September 1939 there were fourteen people detained under the regulation. William Joyce, an extreme fascist and pro-German, was alerted, supposedly by an MI5 officer; he fled to Germany and would be heard of again as the voice of Lord Haw-Haw, through the New British Broadcasting Company, a propaganda arm of the Nazi government. This organisation would figure largely in the case of Admiral Domvile. Joyce's escape caused the Government to speed up other detentions.

Fascist leader, Vidkun Quisling, attempted a seizure of power in Norway when the Nazis invaded the country in May 1940; however he was not accepted by the Nazis. Instead he was put in joint leadership with a German administrator. He would fully cooperate with the Germans including their 'final solution' to destroy the Jews. He would be eventually executed after the war for his collaboration. His name, 'Quisling' would become used as a universal name for traitors. Indeed, the British Admiralty would one day use it of Domvile.

The Norway incident caused further alarm bells to ring in the halls of the British Government. A real fear of a Fascist revolution by Oswald Mosley gripped the Security Service. They carried out a raid on 20 May 1940 at the home of Tyler Kent, an American who had stolen a vast number of papers from the U S Embassy. He had been introduced to Captain Maule Ramsay, an MP and anti-Semite, suspected of links to fascists, by Anna Wolkoff. The files of MI5 note, 'she was on most familiar terms' with Ramsay. She was an extreme pro-Nazi and in constant communication with the traitor, Lord Haw-Haw. Also connected to an Italian Embassy official, Assistant Military attaché Col. Francesco Marigliano, the Duke del Monte, she used him to pass documents through the Belgian embassy. Another intriguing contact she had was Wallace Simpson, the future wife of Edward VIII, who was a client of her couture business. MI5 noted this association in their files on Wolkoff. She was very much at the centre of Tyler's criminal activity and was jailed for ten years. Tyler received seven years. On 22 May 1940, Oswald

Mosley was detained under 18B. There then followed an intense program of detention of fascists and anyone suspected of association with them. By December 1940, more than three thousand had been sent to prison and camps throughout England. These included a great number soldiers, naval and airmen, some arrested whilst on duty, actors, shopkeepers, farmers, writers, churchmen, teachers and even an Artic explorer who had travelled with Shackleton. Both men and women were included in the sweep.

The detention of an individual was without warning and there was no court proceedings involved. An Advisory Committee was set up to which a detainee could appeal but they were not allowed any legal representation or assistance at their appeal hearing. They would not have full details of the reason for their detention or the names of any person associated with giving information that may have led to their detention. Until their appeal was heard they would be kept separate from any other detainee that had already been through the appeal process. Civil liberties groups then, and subsequently, have all condemned 18b for its lack of legal procedure and what was often claimed to be arbitrary detention. This claim was addressed by Norman Birkett in a memo to the Home Office:

> 'The Committee were satisfied that the absence of legal assistance placed the appellant in no real disability, for they regarded it as a duty to assist the appellant to formulate and express the answers he or she desired to make.'

Security Service files contains comments that 'many small fry have been detained, yet many leading figures remain at liberty'. In Oswald Mosley's MI5 secret files, there is a letter from the Prime Minister, referring to these claims and refuting them. However, there probably was a problem for the Government who were aware a number of members of the aristocracy, and even royalty, were known to hold similar views as those of many of the detained.

Chapter 5

A Man Is Known by the Company He Keeps

When the historical files on Admiral Domvile's detention were released in 2002, the 'secret' and 'most secret' MI5 files reveal that the Secret Service was very concerned about the company that he was keeping. It is therefore necessary, as a prelude to what follows, to identify these people and their activities that brought them to the attention of MI5.

The first major figure of concern was Sir Oswald Mosley. An aristocrat, he inherited his father's titles and followed the normal education of his class. He entered the Military Academy at Sandhurst and during the Great War he served in France and later with the Royal Air Corps. He was a Conservative member of parliament from 1918 to 1924 and a Labour member of parliament from 1926 to 1931, with a spell as an Independent in between. It was in 1920 that he married Cynthia Curzon, the daughter of Lord Curzon of Kedleston, the former Viceroy of India. Mosley was very much a part of the higher social class that Domvile delighted to be moving in. Disillusioned with traditional parties not reflecting his right wing views, Mosley founded the New Party which had no electoral success. Influenced by European Fascists, Mosley was a great admirer of Benito Mussolini and went on to found the BUF which included the establishment of a 'protection' wing known as the Blackshirts. This group was based on the *Schutzstaffel* (Protection Squad), the SS of the Nazi system, who also wore black shirts. There was also the Fellowship of the Services which was the secret military organisation connected to BUF and who all were armed.

Mosley's views were anti-Semitic and pro-Nazi and his meetings attracted a great deal of violence. Parallels with Hitler's meetings can be seen, with his thugs also causing trouble. As we have already noted, in 1936 he changed his movement's name to include the term 'National Socialist'. This reflected his support of the Nazi aims for Europe and his aim for a negotiated peace with Hitler. It was believed that following such a peace, a fascist state could be created in England with all immigrants being expelled. In his own words writing in Action on May 23 1940 he said, 'I will continue to do my best to provide people with the possibility of an alternative Government.' This position would form the basis of the charge that he was working secretly to bring revolution to Britain. His friend Domvile would also be tarred with that same brush.

Mosley continually called his Blackshirts on to the streets, especially in the East End where they clashed with large groups of anti-Fascists. He was under the intense scrutiny of the Security Service and their files show their concerns:

> 'The general cry was that the entire population of East London had risen against Mosley and had declared that he and his followers should not pass and that they did not pass owing to the solid front presented by the workers of East London. ... There is abundant evidence that the BUF has been steadily gaining ground in many parts of East London and it has strong support ... There can he no doubt that the unruly element in the crowd was very largely Communist-inspired.'

These activities led to the Public Order Act 1936 as a means to bring a halt to his Blackshirts' activities. Mosley was known to have had affairs and one of these was with the pro-Nazi Diana Mitford, the sister of Unity Mitford. She was an extreme pro-Nazi, like her sister, and was interned during the war. She divorced her first husband to marry Mosley. Mosley had also been married previously to Lady Cynthia Curzon. During that marriage he had affairs with her sister and step-mother. Cynthia died in 1933 which left him free to continue his affair with Diana Mitford. They married in 1936. His closeness to the Nazis was revealed when the marriage was held in secret at the house of the German propaganda minister Joseph Goebbels. There were only six guests present, one of whom was Adolf Hitler. His gift to the newlyweds was a silver framed photograph of himself.

Thus, when war broke out Mosley was seen as a friend of Hitler and to have become a threat to the country. The Security Service had noted that his support in the country was waning and that membership of the BUF had declined from 11,500 in 1939 to 8,600 in 1940. In May 1940 he, along with many supporters of his movement, was interned under Defence Regulation 18B and sent to Brixton prison.

Captain Archibald Henry Maule Ramsay was a Scot and a former army officer injured in the Great War. He too, like Domvile, was a member of the higher social class. He became a member of parliament and was an active and open anti-Semite. He was a great believer in Jewish conspiracy theories and, like Hitler, he refused to accept the *Protocols* as the forgery it was. He admitted making a speech in which he advocated the removal of Jewish influence stating, 'and if we don't do it constitutionally, we'll do it with steel'. In April 1939, the Anglo-German Fellowship organised a grand dinner in honour of *Reichsfrauenfuehrerin* Scholtz-Klink at Claridge's. She had been described by Hitler as the 'perfect Nazi female'. She was Reich's Women's *Führerin* and head of the Nazi Women's League. She was a brilliant speaker and used her time promoting male authority as superior to a woman's status. She expounded the joys of working at home and the importance of child-bearing. Hitler, promoted her as the example of the Aryan woman that all women should follow. People attending the event were Frank Cyril Tiarks (BUF) and Montagu Norman from the Bank of England. Norman was suspected of being a closet Nazi sympathiser because he helped ensure Nazi gold was sold and the money returned to them in 1939. The full facts are buried in the archives of the Bank of International Settlements (BIS) based in Basle, Switzerland. Norman instructed BIS to deduct the gold's value, some $40m (£24m) at 1939 prices, from the Bank of England's account in there. There was also Prince von Bismarck and Geoffrey Dawson, editor of the Times who was a member of the AGF and he forbad any mention of anti-Semitism in Germany, whilst the Nazis were in power pre-war. Many Conservative MPs including Maule Ramsay and Lord Brocket who had attended Hitler's fiftieth birthday celebration and who was a close friend of Joachim von Ribbentrop. Lord Galloway, the Earl of Glasgow, Lord Londonderry, Lord Nuffield, Lord Redesdale, Lord Rennell and the 5th Duke of Wellington were also included. Of course the pro-German Admiral Sir Barry Domvile was at the dinner, mingling with these pro-Nazi friends. One of Scholtz-Klink's many purposes of coming to London was to meet Ramsay and Nazi supporters in secret talks that led to the foundation of the Right Club in 1939. She also met more openly with fascist members of the Nordic League.

The Right Club attracted anti-Semitic Fascists, including the Nazi propagandist Lord Haw-Haw. The concern of the Security Service was Ramsay's fixation with Jewish influence, as he perceived it. The Government believed that if Ramsay felt they were allowing such influence to infect the country, he had contingencies in place for a replacement Government. Indeed, it was to this end that Ramsay sought to have his own people secretly infiltrated into official positions where they could report on any Jewish influences creeping into positions of authority. His attempt at secrecy also led to him taking the name Mr Freeman on certain occasions, to avoid, as he saw it, detection by his Jewish enemies. MI5 were aware of what Ramsay was up to and very concerned about his association with the likes of Mosley and his desire for an alternative Government. Ramsay however always denied that he was a fascist.

He was also connected through the Right Club to Tyler Kent. The Security Service had planted agents at the heart of the Right Club who were monitoring Ramsay's activities. He had gone to Kent's flat on a regular basis to read copies of the stolen American documents. The content of these documents could have compromised the Government and undermined state security. In a matter connected to Kent, Ramsay brought a libel action against the *New York Times*, in which the judge commented that Hitler would call Ramsay a 'friend'. Ramsay, whilst publicly a member of parliament and part of the Establishment, was also conducting secret meetings with many who the Security Service believed to be a threat to the country. The subversive nature of these meetings and reports from agents that confirmed the hostile nature of Ramsay to the Government's policy against Germany, led to an increasing desire to control Ramsay and restrict his activities. Ramsay's continued refusal to be seen to condemn Nazism and his uncertain support for an allied outright victory over Germany, increasingly raised concerns. He was a frequent dining partner of Domvile and was included in many secret meetings which Domvile and Mosley both attended. He too was therefore interned under Defence Regulation 18B and sent to Brixton prison.

Professor A.P. Laurie was a Scottish chemist who took a great interest in paintings and their analysis. He was well respected in academic circles and a member of many of the leading British colleges and academies. His main publications were in the fields of chemistry and materials used in painting. However, in 1939 he published a book entitled *The Case for Germany*. In this he praised Hitler and outlined the Nazi doctrines and polices. He describes Hitler as having:

'… this charming personality, he [Hitler] is of the stern stuff of which leaders of revolutions are made. He stands apart and like all men of genius who have led great movements he is simple and direct, and puzzles and alarms the complex confused personalities of the ordinary diplomatist: yet anyone who will with an open mind study his speeches and watch his actions can learn to understand him. Dwelling among his beloved mountains he makes his decisions and carries them out swiftly and with absolute certainty.'

He continues to praise Hitler and his policies and embraces the anti-Semitic nature of the Nazis. In many ways he was naïve and wrote, 'There will probably be no war in Europe because Hitler and Mussolini stand for Peace'. Laurie's book would play a prominent role in the case against Domvile.

Laurie was among those who founded the Link. What is interesting to note in the founding of the Link are comments from E.D.W. Tennant, founder of the pro-Nazi AGF. He wrote, in his memoirs, 'The Nazis, who possibly expected support from us, were soon disappointed and they encouraged the start of another organisation – the Link – which proved more willing to cooperate with them'. The evidence suggests that this may not be completely true and is an attempt to paint the AGF in a better light after the true nature of the Nazis was exposed by the war. It is hard to understand why the Nazis would prefer an organisation that by and large was composed of the ordinary men and women without influence to one which had many prominent members connected to power. However, it is also true that Ribbentrop and other Nazis welcomed any means to influence British public opinion, which they hoped in turn would bring pressure on the government to favour Germany.

The Link was a vehicle for Domvile's contact and association with the German leaders, pro-Nazis and Fascists, so let us outline exactly what kind of organisation it was. The opening speech of Domvile at Southend made clear what he wanted people to believe – that the Link was not 'anti-anybody and anti-nothing'. He argued the German people had 'found their salvation in Hitler'. He claimed 'to know Hitler personally' and if people knew the real situation, 'they would realise what he [Hitler] had done for Germany'. Domvile would, as we will discover later, always argue that the sole aim of the Link was to encourage friendship with Germany. The question could be asked, that with the AGF already functioning for that purpose, what the need for the Link was. Domvile's answer was that the AGF was an elitist organisation and he wanted to broaden the goal of German/British friendship to the wider population. However, when we look at the origins of the Link, we find that the trio of Laurie, C.E. Carroll and Domvile brought together three very extreme supporters of Germany/Nazism and anti-Semites who appear to want to control their own agenda. These three were joined by Sir John Brown of the British Legion, Susan Fass of the Anglo German *Kameradshaft* and Professor Raymond Beazley. Beazley was a well-known pro-German with Nazi sympathies and was a regular contributor to the *Anglo-German Review*. In fact, all these people had been contributors to the pages of the *Review*. Lord Redesdale, Sir Albert Lambert Ward MP, Captain Edward Unwin VC, Councillor W J Bassett-Lowke, Lord Sempill, A E R Dyer, Archibald Crawford KC and Hubert Maddocks would join in later. As we have seen, Redesdale was extremely pro-Nazi. Lambert Ward was a conservative MP who worked under Chamberlain, whilst Unwin was a war hero being awarded the Victoria Cross for his extreme heroism during action in the Gallipoli peninsula in the First World War. Bassett-Lowke was a model engineer from Northampton and was an importer and supplier of German-made model railways. Lord Sempill was a Scottish Peer and leaned to the far right and fascism. The release of documents from the National Archives would show he was a spy for Japan and Germany and leaked papers to both countries. He was protected from prosecution at the time for reasons that were never entirely clear. Dyer was a pro-Nazi and member of the January Club. Crawford was actively involved in promoting and sustaining the British Empire. Maddocks was a member of the BUF and was considered by Domvile as 'one of Mosley's best men'.

What we learn from this line up is that the Link was keen to present a respectable face but yet have within it a seam of pro-Nazism and Fascism. There was a very loose organisation and its branches began to appear all over the country, including one in Northern Ireland. There is no doubt that in these branches many respectable people were involved. They came from both the Left and Right of politics and included local councillors and civic leaders. There was also a good representation from the various armed services. The activities were almost like any normal civic group with tea-dances, film nights and other social events. However, one thing that differed was in the people who came to speak. Domvile, Carroll and

Laurie would be regulars and often speakers from a German background would take part. Men like Maule Ramsay would appear as would others from a Fascist background. Speakers who were obviously designed to support the Nazi and Fascist agendas included Philip Spranklin, a former BUF member who had joined Goebbels' Munich Foreign Press Office and General Fuller, a BUF member. An unknown MI5 agent reported a speech in 1939 by Fuller and described it as 'pure Goebbels propaganda'.

There was a marked difference in the degree that far right and pro-Nazi activity took place between the urban and rural branches. The branches in and around London were more likely to be involved in pro-German and anti-Semitic activity. Along with Beazley's Birmingham branch there was also the case of Margaret Bothamley who had travelled with Domvile to Germany in 1939. She was an extreme fascist and a member of the International Fascist League as well as the Right Club. She was the Link's organiser in an inner London branch. Aggressively pro-German and anti-Semitic, she travelled around the Link branches promoting her views. She knew she was under the close scrutiny of the Security Service and fled to Germany to become active in broadcasting German propaganda back to England. Bothamley would eventually be returned to England for trial and was sentenced to a term in prison. Domvile's diary notes, 'MB got 12 months – a light sentence I feel'. The 28 March 1946 diary page has a copy of *The Times*' report of the sentence glued to it. It is also interesting to note that Domvile is asked by Bothamley's sister in 1948 to sort and look after her 'papers'. This all suggests a very close relationship between the two and it was suggested she may indeed have been one of his lovers.

The Acton branch was organised by Eric Whittleton who was an active anti-Semite and who from the mid-'thirties, regularly made statements against Jews and their influence as he saw it. Whittleton was a regular subscriber to the *Patriot*, where he would argue for a move from democracy to a government that would oppose 'Organised Jewry'. The distribution of pro-Nazi and anti-Semitic literature would often surface at Link meetings and occasionally similar literature would find its way into mailings from the Link offices.

On 21 December 1937, concerns were raised in parliament about the Link by John Parker Labour MP for Romford:

'I would like to draw attention also to an organisation called "The Link," which nominally exists for the purpose of promoting Anglo-German friendship, but in reality is a camouflaged Fascist organisation. The founders are Admiral Sir Barry Domvile, and Professor A.P. Laurie, who is perhaps the most persistent pro-Fascist letter-writer to the newspapers in this country. I would like to quote some of the remarks of Sir Barry Domvile when inaugurating a branch of "The Link" in Southend: Fascism might not be a system of government which suited this country but it suited Germany very well. We must not be on opposite sides to Germany in any future war. The Link was in touch with all big German organisations. On the question of Colonies he said that the British Government must face up to that issue whatever that might mean. I think that when you have an organisation like "The Link," with many distinguished people connected with it, carrying on propaganda on behalf of foreign countries here, the matter ought to be investigated by the Government.'

And in a discourse between Sir Geofrey Manders and Samuel Hoare:

'On 30th March 1939 Geoffrey Manders asked the Secretary of State for the Home Department whether he is aware of the activities of a pro-Nazi organisation in this country known as the Link; whether his attention has been called to certain methods of propaganda adopted; and whether he will take steps to deport the German subjects concerned?

The Secretary of State for the Home Department Sir Samuel Hoare:

'I understand that the organisers and principal officials of this body are all British subjects. The last part of the question does not, therefore, arise.

'Mr. Mander

'Is the right hon. Gentleman aware that this organisation does all it can to glorify Hitlerism, and derives support from Nazi sources; and is it not desirable that the British public should realise what its precise but undeclared objects are?

'Sir S. Hoare

'I understand that this organisation is mainly for the purposes of pro-Nazi and anti-Semite propaganda. More than that I do not know.'

As we will see later, concerns were also raised that the Link was receiving money from Germany to support its existence.

Through the Link, Laurie and Domvile and those noted above were regularly in contact. Laurie was also connected to the Fascists and Mosley held him in high esteem. In the secret MI5 files, Mosley described him as 'a great intellectual and a very difficult man to handle'. He also states that Laurie had 'violent opinions, but a perfectly honest Englishman, I should think myself'. He confirmed that Laurie was 'pro-German instead of pro-British'. However, Mosley says of Laurie, 'in private life he is the mildest man alive'.

Cola Ernest Carroll became a journalist and edited the British Legion's newspaper. The RFC was the forerunner of the RAF and it was here that Carroll would have had his first contact with Oswald Mosley. In 1936, he founded the *Anglo-German Review* as a publication to foster links between Britain and Germany. In many ways this was simply a pro-German paper, but in 1939 it took a more concerning turn. Carroll began to move sharply towards anti-Semitism proving himself to be a virulent anti-Semitic, echoing much of what Mosley and Ramsay believed. In April 1937, he was particularly concerned with the main-stream press taking an anti-German tone. He used the *Review* to attack Jewish criticism of what the Nazis were doing in Germany. He argued they had no right to use the British press for 'vicious propaganda' and maintained the Fascist belief that the British press was controlled by Jews. He berated them for 'stirring up trouble with a friendly neighbour'. The *Review* continued in this vein and as the readership continued to grow and the letters page showed support, it has to be concluded that the readership was in agreement with the editorial team. He also published excerpts from Hitler's speeches, especially those calling for a relationship with Britain, along with articles from Goebbels. Domvile also contributed articles. Carroll was a close friend of Walter Hewel, a confidant of Hitler on foreign affairs and he was a strong advocate for the appeasement of Hitler and found a common purpose with Domvile.

In 1946, he joined Laurie and Domvile, to establish the Link. He and Domvile became close friends. In MI5 files, Carroll was seen as a 'charming' man, who was a suspected danger to national security at the outbreak of war. Guy Liddell records in his diary that Carroll had handed in a complete list of the Link members to the police but he suspected that he had already got rid of any incriminating evidence. Carroll was sent to Brixton under Defence Regulation 18B.

Robert Gordon-Canning, a product of Eton, was a Great War hero winning the Military Medal. From a military family, he had pretensions to greatness and claimed descent from Lord Byron, the poet, whom he said was his great-grandfather. However, there is no proof of this claim. Following the war, he became a passionate advocate of the Arab cause and anti-Jewish in his views. He strongly disagreed with Government policy on the Middle East and supported Arab claims to territory in Morocco and elsewhere. He was a committed Fascist and joined Mosley in the BUF. He was also Mosley's best man at the secret wedding in Germany. He boasted of having had meetings and dinners with Hitler and other Nazi leaders. However, in 1939, disagreement with Mosley caused him to leave him and join other Fascist groups. He then became a member of the Right Club and the Link. After the war he would confirm his devotion to Hitler by purchasing a marble bust of him in a sale of artefacts from the German Embassy in London for £500 (£20,000 in 2016) and comparing Hitler to Jesus Christ. He was increasingly dissatisfied with how the government was approaching war with Germany and began to hold meetings at his flat with leading Fascist figures. The Security Service were monitoring his activities and became alarmed at reports that a Fascist plot was being hatched at these meetings. He regularly dined with Domvile and attended secret meetings with him. The Government decided to put him Brixton under Defence Regulation 18B.

The authorities were also concerned that the Admiral was connected to Henry Luttman-Johnson, a Scottish landowner and former cavalry officer in the Indian Army; Domvile's diaries show Luttman-Johnson would regularly send Scottish salmon to him. He also moved in the higher social order in Britain. He was among the founders of the January Club, which included Mosley, Carroll and Gordon-Canning. The club also had many MP's, aristocrats and high ranking military among its members. The activities of the club also concerned the Security Service. Along with others he was involved in the Information and Policy Group, a forum that on the surface was a discussion group on farming and agriculture but its real purpose was to discuss how to promote pro-German propaganda. It produced a regular newspaper. Luttman-Johnson was also detained in Brixton under the provisions of Defence Regulation 18B.

The MI5 files reveal a number of other minor characters and organisations connected to Admiral Domvile and who raised concerns. People like Olive Baker a close associate of his, who was given five years penal servitude for spreading pro-German propaganda. Baker worked as a teacher in Germany returning to this country in 1939. Whilst awaiting trial in prison she cut her wrists and used her blood to write Heil Hitler and Heil Mosley on the cell wall. There was Norah Elam, known as Dacre Fox, who was a Fascist activist and pro-German. She stood for parliament as an independent, without success. Guy Liddell noted in his diary that she was under the scrutiny of the Security Service and was suspected of being a link in a money chain from the Nazis to the BUF. Liddell linked her to Peter Whinfield, the son of Colonel H G Whinfield, a BUF candidate in an election. He was arrested in Switzerland as part of this money link. A sum of £10,000 [£390,000 2016] was received by Elam, as a 'donation'. There was also a 'special' account MI5 knew about that was being used to supply funds to specific BUF finance controllers. Whinfield admitted his Gestapo connections and gave names of those in England with whom he was associated. Special Branch raided Elam's offices and found a power of attorney in certain matters from Oswald Mosley. This turned the focus of MI5 on Elam's associates including Admiral Domvile. Another association of concern was with the British Council for Christian Settlement in Europe, a front for promoting peace with Germany and the acceptance of the Nazis to remain in power.

It is reasonable to point out that all these characters were from the higher reaches of British society. The British monarchy was descended from German ancestry and there were many links to them from other members of the aristocracy. Therefore, we do find that very important dukes and duchesses such as Lord and Lady Russell of Liverpool and Arthur Charles Wellesley, 5th Duke of Wellington, involved in far right activities. The secret files of MI5 are littered with references to other such figures being connected to Nazism, Mosley and other fascist groupings. There was in Britain a substantial minority of opinion that wanted to avoid any conflict with Germany.

It was against this background that the Government decided to act against the Domviles and their son.

Chapter 6

The Reasons for the Domviles' Detention

The secret papers released in 2002, show that the Security Service had major concerns about the Domviles. They were not the only ones; the Admiral's former colleagues were also alarmed at his activities and connections. In a very direct letter, in June 1940, Richard Carter of Naval Intelligence wrote to the Security Service:

'The Admiralty view is that if there be any British "Quislings", then there are few more likely candidates for the role than Admiral Domvile and his wife and we should feel distinctly happier if these two were finally out of harm's way.'

Papers were drawn up which framed the case for detention under Defence Regulation 18B Regulation. These set out in detail the reasons for their detention.

The introduction was couched in the vague terms of the regulations, stating that the detention was that they had been 'recently concerned in acts prejudicial to public safety and the defence of the realm'. There then followed a list of specifics for Admiral Domvile. He was:

    I. Founder and stable of the Link. The charge was that Domvile was the one who was at the centre of the Link and without whom it would never had continued.
    II. Was closely associated with prominent Nazi leaders in Germany and in this country
    III. Is sympathetic to Germany and the Nazi system of Government
    IV. Has been closely associated with Sir Oswald Mosley and other prominent leaders of the BUF
    V. Has been active in the furtherance of the objects of the BUF
    VI. Has since the outbreak of war discussed with Sir Oswald Mosley and other prominent members of the BUF the coordination of fascist activities and the achievement of fascist revolution in this country

These allegations were expanded in accompanying notes to describe Domvile as pro-German, spreading German propaganda through the Link meetings. He was also noted to have visited Germany and had been 'entertained by Hitler, Himmler, Goebbels and a number of prominent Nazis'. The Security Service believed the Admiral was 'wholeheartedly' behind the promotion of pro-German views and even had become 'anti-British' in his outlook. They also quoted from a letter written by Otto Georg Gustav Karlowa, a Nazi diplomat working in England, to all German's at the Embassy in London and to the leaders of all German groups throughout Britain:

'I have promised Admiral Domvile that we will take part and will see that young ladies attend as dancing partners. We wish to take part in this gathering of the Link and I request you to take energetic steps to see that it is done.'

This, it was suggested, showed that the Admiral was involved with Nazis in promoting the Link. He had also published an article in the German newspaper *Berliner Tageblatt* supporting Germany's claim to retake the colonies. In his diary on 31 January 1938 Domvile's comment on the article was, 'looks fine'.

Furthermore, he wrote an introduction for Laurie's book *The Case for Germany*, and thus was seen to support Laurie's positive views of Hitler and his policies. The book was also being distributed in many pro-German countries to promote a case against Britain and her government. The belief in Whitehall was that Domvile's name being associated with such a book gave an impression that the British navy itself supported the book's viewpoint.

His alleged involvement in the Information and Policy Group was also cited and it was claimed that this was the disguised revival of the now defunct Link. The Security Service was convinced that Domvile was 'a moving spirit' behind the British Council for Christian Settlement in Europe wanting appeasement with Nazi Germany. The basis for these claims came from various sources including agents that had infiltrated the BUF and the Link.

As with all detainees under the Regulation 18B, Domvile was not shown any of the allegations or 'evidence' for his detention. He could appeal to an Advisory Committee to ask for a review. In that situation he could not have any legal representation nor could he ask any question as to the sources for the case against him. He would also not be told of the committee's recommendation to the Home Secretary as to whether he should be freed or remain in detention. He would eventually appeal to this committee after initially seeking a writ of habeas corpus and abandoning that approach, when it became clear that Regulation 18B would deny that route.

Domvile's activities had not only drawn attention to himself, it also brought the official spotlight on his whole family. Lady Domvile because of her connections to Germany through her father already had been suspected of pro-German sympathies. That was the very first question that was asked of her when she attended an appeals hearing on the October 22 1940. She confirmed that her English mother had 'become German' on marriage but took back her 'British nationality' on the death of her husband. That was when Lady Domvile was seven. She confirmed that she had been to Germany 'three or four years ago' and had met some of the German leaders and had dinner with Himmler and Lord Londonderry and his daughters. She acknowledged knowing Mosley and confirmed she was a BUF member. She had dined with him and his wife but she tried to distance herself from him politically. The committee presented her with a number of names of fascists and pro-Germans which she either denied knowing of had very little knowledge of them. She had supported her husband in Link matters but was not active. She referred often to illnesses preventing her for being so. When asked about Mosley and his being pro-Nazi, she refused to accept that he was in any way inclined to Nazism. After this first hearing the committee wrote to G St C Pilcher of MI5 saying that 'the case against her simply does not exist'. Further evidence was needed if they were to recommend her continued detention.

She was brought back before the appeals committee on November 5 1940 where she was challenged on the claims made against her. She presented the face of a woman who could not remember certain things that had been reported to the authorities, such as meetings with known fascists. Specifically on meetings with Mosley, she was presented with a number of times she had met and dined with him. Initially she denied this but presented with evidence from her diaries where she had made entries of the meetings she then back peddled to say they were not significant.

When asked if she was politically active and had been so with Mrs Muriel Whinfield another BUF member, she said 'No. I did not definitely. I have done nothing in the way of active work such as leaflets or propaganda or selling the paper. I promise you I have not'. This was not true. She had actively supported Whinfield when she stood as a BUF candidate in an election. Further pressed with evidence, she would say, 'I honestly cannot remember that'. As to meetings at her home, despite the reports from the agent's wife, they never happened.

On closer inspection she was found to be an ardent supporter of Mosley and joined the BUF. She also flirted with other right wing groups and often entertained Fascist ladies groups at her home. One of these ladies was in fact the wife of an MI5 agent (unnamed in the MI5 files), who was reporting back to her husband the contents of the meetings. She was therefore held in detention for another year being finally released in November 1941.

Compton Domvile was also suspected of fascist and pro-German sympathies. He had briefly joined the navy like his father but had left after a brief time. He suffered from sleeping sickness and that may have been the cause of his leaving. He was a member of the BUF and had met Mosley and other leading figures through their association with his parents. He had travelled to Germany on occasions and had met some of the leaders, particularly Himmler. He was taken to an interrogation centre at Ham Common rather than to a prison. It was not a pleasant experience for him: 'It was not long before my memory began to deteriorate. Certain periods of my life completely disappeared from my mind'. Whilst no physical torture was inflicted on detainees here, they were placed on a starvation diet and prevented from sleeping for long periods. With his illness Compton would have suffered particularly badly. His detention record has been found to be missing and unavailable for inspection.

Admiral Domvile's other two children were not detained. His daughter Miranda was investigated but she was found not to have been influenced by her parents and served in a government department during the war. Domvile's son, Barry junior, was serving as a second lieutenant with the army in Jerusalem. In early June, MI5 were concerned as to where his loyalties lay, bearing in mind his various family members' views. His commanding officer sent a report back stating that he had observed no problems with him and that he was behaving satisfactorily. In an interview with him, Domvile's son said, 'I am single-minded in my attitude to the king.' He would eventually be declared missing, presumed killed in action in Crete in June 1941.

Let us now turn to a review of the known facts around the Domviles.

Chapter 7

Domvile's Activity and MI5's Records

It was in February 1935 that Cola Carroll discussed with Schwedler of the Trans-Ocean News Service (also Transocean News Service) the idea of an Anglo-German newssheet funded by the Germans. Transocean was originally a *bona-fide* news agency in Berlin. When the Nazi party took over it became an arm of their propaganda machine. Carroll had worked for Transocean It was in 1936 when the financing of the news sheet was again raised. Finance would be received from Germany through 'advertising'. On October 1936, Carroll met with Otto Karlowa, the Nazi diplomat in London, for further discussions. In March 1937, Herr Durchiem of the German Ribbentrop Bureau, wrote to Karl Marhau of the German Chamber of Commerce expressing his greatest satisfaction at how the new sheet was run, 'It was the first paper brought out by an Englishman which published the truth in our sense.' Carroll was also in touch with Dr Erich Hetzler of the Ribbentrop Bureau and in a letter on 1 February 1939 he wrote, 'The membership [of the Link] is increasing slowly but very steadily. It has a deficit of about £5 per week [£300 in 2016], which has so far been covered by the *Review*.'

Again, on 29 March 1939, he wrote to the Financial Director of the Bureau, 'I am venturing to bother you in this matter because we are faced with meeting heavy commitments before Easter, that is to say early next week, and since failure to meet them would jeopardise the existence of both the *Review* and the Link.' In May, he received £200 [£12,000 in 2016] from the Bureau.

Between October 1936 and July 1937 world events were moving on. Japan had invaded Manchuria and Italy had invaded Ethiopia. Both these countries also signed a treaty with Nazi Germany; the Japanese treaty was specifically against Russia. Japan also invaded China. Against this background Britain was becoming more concerned about her territories and the rise of Nazi influence. The Secret Service continued to watch all those who had any degree of sympathy with Germany. MI5 raised the question about

Domvile's German born wife and her brother's earlier activity in 1937 when he had been 'engaged in espionage activity'. The Admiralty also had sent a message to Domvile through his brother that they were 'getting very concerned about Admiral Domvile and his association with the Link'. It was in November of that year that Domvile wrote to a contact he called 'Hefferman' in Munich. He expressed his gratitude 'for all the work you are doing for THE LINK' and hoping he would live to see it 'bear real fruit'. Domvile's diary also records a meeting with Max von Rogiste of Munich at his home in Roehampton. This entry, and others, shows that Domvile was regularly meeting Germans and was aware of the downside of Nazism: 'The first time I had seen the bad side of Nazi-dom.'

The Domviles were therefore still very much under suspicion.

In March 1938, Domvile wrote to Heinrich Himmler (*Reichsführer* of the *Schutzstaffel* – SS) introducing him to Cola Carroll and told him that Carroll, '… is one of the best workers in this country for friendship with Germany and his paper is most successful in furthering this object.' He goes on to confirm that the *Anglo-German Review* is the 'publicity organ of THE LINK' and expresses Carroll's hopes 'of obtaining certain official facilities for his paper'. He asks Himmler to be of assistance to Carroll for which 'I shall be very grateful'. We know from the records of the Security Service discussed above that these 'facilities' were the giving of cash through the medium of advertising.

In April 1938, an article appeared in *World Review* and repeated in the Australian press where Domvile was critical of the UK's Government policy towards Japan. On 29 September of that year the Munich Agreement was signed by Chamberlain along with France and Italy giving the Sudetenland to Germany from the Czechoslovak Republic. This was a great moment for Domvile and those in England who were working for peace with Germany through the appeasement of Hitler. Twenty days later he called a meeting of the Link in Portsmouth titled 'Anglo-German Relations'. Professor Laurie would be there to talk about his book *The Case for Germany* and they had a member who was 'present in Czechoslovakia during the crisis'. Domvile would later deny knowing about the contents of *The Case for Germany*. Is it conceivable that when giving a talk on the book, Laurie would not mention its contents? In October 1938, Domvile along with others wrote to *The Times* supporting Chamberlain; it was published on the 6th.

'TO THE EDITOR OF *THE TIMES*
'The undersigned who believe that real friendship and co-operation between Britain and Germany are essential to the establishment of enduring peace not only in Western Europe but throughout the world, strongly deprecate the attempt which is being made to sabotage an Anglo-German rapprochement by distorting the facts of the Czecho-Slovak settlement.

'We believe that the Munich Agreement was nothing more than the rectification of one of the most flagrant injustices of the Peace Treaty. It took nothing from Czecho-Slovakia to which that country could rightly lay claim, and gave nothing to Germany which could have been rightfully withheld. We see in the policy so courageously pursued by the Prime Minister [Neville Chamberlain] the end of a long period of lost opportunities and the promise of a new era to which the tragic years that have gone since the War will seem like a bad dream.

'Signed by:
'Lord Arnold, Captain Bernard Ackworth, Prof. Sir Raymond Beazley, Mr. C.E Carroll, Sir. John Smedley Crooke, M.P., Mr. W.H. Dawson, Admiral Sir, Barry Domvile, Mr. A.E.R Dyer, Lord Fairfax of Cameron, Viscount Hardinge of Penshurst, Mr. F.C Jarvis, Mr. Douglas Jerrold, Sir. John Latta, Prof. A.P Laurie, The Marquess of Londonderry, Vice-Admiral V.B Molteno, Captain A.H Maule Ramsey, M.P., Mr. Wilmot Nicholson, Lord Redesdale, Captain Lane-Fox Pitt-Rivers, Capt. Arthur Rogers, OBE, Maj-Gen, Arthur Solly-Flood, Mrs. Nesta Webster, Mr. Bernard Wilson.'

Domvile's diary suggests that the letter originated from the offices of the Link and was composed by him. He notes about the letter, 'Went well'. Domvile had originated the letter and gathered signatures from more respectable members of society in order to cover the more unsavoury names; Carroll, Beazley, Dyer, Redesdale, Pitt-Rivers, Laurie, Ramsay, Nicolson, Londonderry, Mount, Dawson, Arnold, Smedley-Crooke and Webster were all well-known pro-Germans, Fascists and pro-Nazis. As a result, *The Times* was reluctant to publish the letter, both on the grounds of unease with appeasement and the fact that the signatories were connected with the far Right and Fascism.

On 21 December 1938, at the opening of a branch of the Link in Wells, Somerset Domvile again spoke on the need of a good relationship with Germany and appears to be in sympathy with Hitler's reaction to the Versailles Treaty and his action against Czechoslovakia. A 'Most Secret' report by MI5 on Domvile's diary on 2 February 1939 gave the Security Service's opinions on the admiral. In it, they describe Domvile as not being of 'first class importance to Germans except as a contact man' and that they use him to 'make propaganda among the right people'. His character is described:

'He is enormously enamoured of all Germans. A great snob. An anti-Semite, pro-Franco, thinks Mosley magnificent, Hitler a marvel, Gregarious; enjoys German Embassy dinners to the full; enjoys seeing his letters in the Press, enjoys wearing decorations, enjoys being busy; Of no great intellectual ability. Drinks too much; has mistresses.'

Professor Charles Saroléa, a Belgian teaching at Edinburgh University, was a speaker at a meeting of the Link on 25 February 1939. Saroléa was a right-winger, anti-Semitic, pro-Franco and a Nazi Government supporter; in many respects a suitable bed-fellow for Domvile. He had welcomed many Nazis who visited Scotland pre-war. He had also visited Germany on numerous occasions and was invited to the Nuremberg rallies, being given the 'best seat in the house'. It is therefore no surprise that in his address at the Link meeting he was supportive of Hitler and his actions. Domvile did not contradict Saroléa but simply added that, '… friendship with Germany was made difficult by the many persecutions and expulsions; but these were only symptoms of the revolutionary period in Germany's recent history.' He then went on to criticise the British approach of allowing Jews to enter Palestine and upsetting the 'Moslems and Arabs'. Two nights later he was speaking at Leeds, again supporting peace with Germany and showing sympathy to Hitler's reaction to the Versailles Treaty. He notes in his diary on the day of this meeting, 'Everywhere I go I am asked about the Jews. What are we going to do about them?'

In March 1939, Hitler occupied further areas of Czechoslovakia, raising more concern in Britain, who, along with France, guaranteed the borders of Poland. In the following month Carroll was writing to Dr Hetzler in Berlin asking him to ask 'the Fuhrer to invite Admiral Sir Barry Domvile' to the Nazi 'Party Day'. In the following month, Fascist Italy invaded Albania. The tension throughout Europe was very high as the growth of expansionism of Germany and Italy were watched with apprehension. In England, concern was reaching a high level in government circles.

The activities of the Fascists and pro-Germans were attracting even greater interest from the Security Service who in turn made the Prime Minister aware of their anxieties. In August 1939, it was raised in parliament by the Home Secretary, Sir Samuel Hoare:

> 'The professed object of this organisation [the Link] is to promote understanding between England and Germany, but it does nothing to enable Germans to understand the English view, and devotes itself to expressing the German point of view. The information I have [from MI5] shows that the organisation is being used as an instrument of the German propaganda service and that money has been received from Germany by one of the active organisers [Carroll]. As regards the last part of the question, I have no power to intervene unless an organisation breaks the law.'

This statement became a major newspaper story with large bold headlines in papers across the whole of the country. Domvile's name appeared prominently and the Link now was connected with German propaganda. One example was the Edinburgh Evening News which bore the headline:

> 'DISCLOSURES ABOUT "THE LINK" Activities of Anglo-German Body'

Beneath the headline, the newspaper related the details of the Link's formation and its aim to promote links between Germany and Britain. It reported that the claim of German finance was 'based upon the most accurate information', without knowing that the source was MI5. The Admiral was on a visit to Salzburg to promote the Ring, a version of the Link in Germany. He was seated in 'Herr Hitler's Box at the Salzburg Festival'.

Domvile was enraged when he heard the reports and spent a day on the phone from Salzburg to newspapers in Britain, denying Hoare's claims and insisting the Link was not financed by German money. On his return, he, along with Laurie and Carroll, set about giving press conferences to deny the claims.

The *Leeds Mercury* ran its story with Domvile offering to close the Link if the Government did not want people like him 'establishing friendly feelings and relations between two great nations'. Laurie acknowledges that some members do get payments for articles and books as he himself had done because British publishers would not publish his book. The constant defence was that the Link was simply an organisation that wanted to build understanding with Germany. However, the British press, and indeed it would appear public opinion, were not prepared to accept that view. An example was an editorial in the *Sunderland Daily Echo* which concluded:

'The trouble with the Link – and other groups like it, such as The Anglo-German Fellowship – is that invariably such societies are founded in Britain with the genuine and originally commendable desire to obtain 'understanding' with Germany, but that sooner or later such bodies become propagandist tools of Berlin's publicity machine.'

As we will see later, German funding was a topic for discussion before the appeals committee. The newspapers began to print letters from Link members who were resigning. One, Alison Outhwaite, wrote to the *Daily Express*:

'I joined because Sir Barry Domvile is a personal friend. The first meeting I went to was last November in a South Kensington hotel. A parson was in the chair. A young Englishman spoke who announced that he had worked for the German Propaganda Ministry doing broadcasts from Munich. He ranted for one hour against our freedom of the press, and extolled the German press and the German Government. Anti-Semitic pamphlets and literature of the Friends of Franco-Spain were handed round.'

The *Portsmouth Evening Herald* carried a report from Captain Gosson, a retired army officer, who had founded the Link branch in Portsmouth, on his resignation and suggestions to Sir Barry to close the Link.

The *Star* reported on a visit to Berlin by the vice-Chairman of the Leeds branch of the Link, Mr Dickenson. He had written back to the secretary of the branch urging immediate disbandment. He was alarmed by conversations he had with German SS officers in an Anglo-German Club, where the secretary of the club 'practically admitted that the Link was an integral part of the German propaganda system'. He also spoke of the secretary of the German Economic and Political Organisation in Berlin and 'he confessed that the Link was a branch of the Propaganda Ministry and that it would not exist without the permission and the assistance of the German Government'. The *Daily Express* also commented on the photographs of Domvile with Himmler 'very smart in his uniform' taken in Germany. The *Jewish Chronicle* complained of anti-Semitic pamphlets distributed at the North-West London branch of the Link. Domvile was appearing in these newspapers frantically denying and refuting any charges against the Link but without offering any substantive evidence to support his claims. On 7 August 1939, once again in Portsmouth, Domvile and Carroll joined Professor Laurie for the announcement of *The Case for Germany* now being accepted for printing in Italy on behalf of a German publisher. No British publisher would accept it. Laurie refuted claims that the Italian publisher was pro-Nazi, although Germany would be the main place for distribution of the book. He confirmed that he had received £150 (£9000 in 2016) from the publisher. This in itself was interesting as this sum was three times what would normally have been paid at that time. It suggests that the book was of great importance to Germany in its propaganda war. We again see Domvile present at the announcement of a book he claimed he never read.

On the declaration of war on 9 September 1939, Domvile closed down the Link:

'The Link is closed down on the declaration of war. That was essential. The King's enemies become our enemies. We have done our best for better Anglo-German relations and with the outbreak of hostilities there was no more to be done. All the branches are closed.'

A number of reports in the newspapers pointed to some of Link members being detained.

Although this public statement suggested Domvile was severing any links with pro-Germans and Fascists ('the King's enemies') the truth was that he was still involved. The Security Service was aware of two letters from Domvile to Luttman-Johnson, connected to the pro-German groups, Information and Policy and Christian Settlement in Europe. The first letter on 13 September 1939 was to invite him to a meeting in London at Captain Gordon-Canning's flat. Canning, an extreme fascist and pro-German wanted an accommodation with Hitler. The second letter, on 24 September, to Luttman-Johnson, who did not come to the meeting because he was in Scotland, confirms the meeting happened and comments, 'the meeting was a great success' and names those attending as Drummond, Canning, Carroll and others, all pro-German and Fascists. In the first letter, Domvile also expressed the opinion that the war was opposed to the best interests of the Empire. He referred to small pro-German groups, such as Information and Policy, and told Luttman-Johnson that he wanted to 'rope them all in'. His view expressed in that letter claimed that Germany had 'checkmated' the government. The letters to Luttman-Johnson were of great concern and formed part of the case against Domvile. The letters stated, 'I am having some very interesting negotiations with Oswald Mosley Ramsay and Norman Hay ... Our plans are maturing well.'

Hay was the editor of the pro-German group Information and Policy which we have already noted was a means for German propaganda in Britain.

These comments do seem to implicate Domvile in some sort of 'plan' involving three pro-German fascists. Domvile in his diary writes of this meeting on 19 September 1936, 'A new Council formed. Pudd [his wife] and I are on it' and of the meeting states, 'what might become an important meeting'. It is therefore not surprising that by late September 1939, the Special Branch were particularly alarmed by the activity of the Right Club in England. Captain Ramsay and his club were under the closest observation by MI5. A letter from MI5 of 22 September 1939 carried a warning:

'The activity of the pro-Fascist and anti-Semitic Right Club, of which he [Captain Ramsay] is the leader, is centred principally upon the contacting of sympathisers, especially among officers in the Armed Forces, and by the spreading by personal talks of the Club's ideals. The talk has now reached the stage of suggestions that a military *coup d'état* is feasible.'

On 1 November 1939, Domvile wrote a letter to Carroll which also raised suspicions at MI5. In it he wrote, 'I have a lot to tell you that I cannot write.'

The newspapers were now filled with anger at those who were pro-German, appeasers or pacifists. Domvile could not be in any doubt about the mood of the country nor the terrible conditions in Poland after the Nazi invasion. One report in the *Hastings and St Leonard's Gazette* serves as an example:

> 'Half the world pleaded with them. Wantonly the Nazi authorities rejected the plea and set their military machine in motion. Warsaw is in ruins. Poland has ceased to exist. She has joined Czechoslovakia in the blood sacrifice demanded by the insatiable devils of domination.'

It was also on 1 November 1939 that Domvile wrote to Olive Baker and referred to 'these hard luck stories of lying Jews', which added to the charge of anti-Semitism against him. The Security Service was also aware of a letter of 9 November from Domvile to Luttman-Johnson. In this letter he wrote:

> 'Many thanks for yours. CEC [Cola Carroll] is OK. Give us the address. Be careful of anyone called Drummond, not the bulldog breed. There is a lot of agent provocateurs going on. True to form the Government is frightened. Many details in a paper coming out tomorrow, Information and Policy. We have regular meetings once a fortnight, about a dozen of us discuss the situation. I wish you could come and meet old friends.'

A security service report from an MI5 agent who was employed by Mosley's BUF 'since its inception', reported on these meetings. He reported that both Sir Barry and Lady Domvile (who was also a member of the 'inner circle' of the BUF) had attended the meetings and the 'conversation was little short of treasonable'. MI5 reported on a letter of 5 December 1939 when Domvile wrote to Carroll. He had written:

> 'I am not in B.C.C.S [British Council for Christian Settlement in Europe] though always ready to help unofficially. It does them no good if I join because the press call it a disguised Link ... I lunched with Gordon-Canning [a leading Fascist] last week and Newsham [Editor of *Truth* – a British nationalist newspaper] was there.'

This again caused concern and indicated that Domvile who had stated that he had given up the Link activities was in fact still active. The Security

Service used this as evidence that Domvile was acting against British interests and thus deserved to be detained in Brixton.

As Christmas 1939 approached, there could be no misunderstanding about Germany's actions and the cruelty which Hitler was afflicting on occupied territories. Newspapers filled columns with accounts and the word 'holocaust' was beginning to be used. The *Express and Echo* was graphic:

> 'The murder of St Stephen, the massacre of the innocents, the holocaust of Poland, the torpedoing of merchant ships, the prospect of children gasping for life … Quite apart from actual war, there was enough to make the angels weep before Hitler brewed his hell's broth.'

Britain was in no mood for pro-German sympathisers. Against this backdrop, Lady Domvile on 28 December 1939 wrote to a Fascist friend of 'the coming year which I hope one prays will be a year of fulfilment for BUF'. The following day, a Special Branch officer sat down to write a letter to MI5, which he initials ASN. It was regarding the Domviles' son, Compton. The letter noted that he had left the Royal Naval College 'but the reason for his leaving was not known'. What was known was that Compton Domvile was due to be called up for military training and was to report for a medical examination on 4 January 1940. However, he had 'boasted he will obtain exemption from such training, on medical grounds, by producing false certificates'. The writer reports that Compton is 'a friend of Oswald Mosley' and had said that he had 'received letters from Germany via Switzerland, from Unity Mitford'. The letter stated that Compton had travelled widely in Germany and had stayed with Himmler and other Nazi leaders. 'He was also active with his father in the work of the Link'. The letter ended by accusing him of being a German sympathiser and was 'a danger to this country'. He would eventually be detained under 18B. The remainder of December of 1939 saw continuing press coverage of the 'holocaust in Europe' and the news of the establishment of concentration camps and of the ill-treatment of Jews by the Nazis. Whilst the use of 'holocaust' by the press at this time concerned the terrible destruction in Europe, the word would later take on a more sinister meaning when the Nazis moved from the harassment and detention of Jews to their 'final solution' in 1942.

January 1940 saw Sir Barry writing more letters, one to Kenneth Duffield, who he later claimed he did not know nor could he remember writing to him.

In that letter, Domvile used phrases that again caused concern with the Security Service, for example, 'I am in close touch with Oswald Mosley … our plans are maturing well.' In another letter he had written, 'I am having some interesting negotiations with Sir Oswald Mosley, Captain Ramsay and Mr Norman Hay.'

In January, Naval Intelligence were concerned about the admiral writing to the pro-Fascist *Truth* newspaper. In December of 1939 he had complained in one about Churchill calling the German navy 'baby killers' and appeared to offer support to the German seaman involved. Three readers had responded attacking Domvile and quoting specific instances when the German navy had attacked unmanned ships including a hospital ship and they had also bombarded Scarborough civilians. Naval intelligence felt strongly that Domvile 'approved of such attacks'. They further accused him of being a propagandist for Germany and believed he should be 'controlled' using the 18B Defence Regulations.

Further observations of Oswald Mosley by MI5 found him holding a 'secret meeting' on 7 February 1940 with Fascists and among the attendees was Admiral Domvile. This meeting is confirmed in Domvile's diary entry for that day. MI5 also reported that Lady Domvile was attending fortnightly meetings of 'the inner cabinet' of Mosley's BUF and that she was paying 'the most prominent portion' of the salary of a BUF activist called Hammond. Further concern was raised by a letter from Lord Tavistock that was personally signed by him and sent to a number of people, including Domvile. It read:

'Dear Domvile,

'In view of a most important development which gives grounds for a belief that the war could be immediately ended on reasonable terms, on which I have already been in touch with the Government, I am most anxious to have your advice.

'I would greatly value it if you could attend a small strictly private meeting here (Belgrave Square) on Tuesday February the 13th at 2.45pm, when I will place information before you for your consideration and discussion.

'Yours sincerely
'Tavistock'

This letter was written against a background of Tavistock's pro-German sympathies. MI5 were monitoring him and their files reflect their great concerns:

> 'Throughout the winter of 1939/40 he was actively engaged in propaganda which had as its object a negotiated peace. This propaganda was undertaken through the medium of the British Council for Christian Settlement in Europe. In the early part of 1940 Lord Tavistock, as the Duke of Bedford then was, travelled to Ireland to establish contact with the German Government through the German Legation in Dublin with a view to negotiating peace terms. So obsessed with his aims has he become that he publicly blames the British Government for the war, makes excuses for Hitler and for Nazi methods and atrocities and maintains that the only hope for this country lies in a negotiated peace.'

They gave their frank opinion about Tavistock:

> 'Having regard to the known sympathies of the Duke, he is a person who, if there was an invasion of this country, would be likely to cause alarm and despondency by public utterances and to weaken the will of his countrymen to resist the invader. In the event of the Duke falling into the hands of the enemy he would be likely to be set up as a *gauleiter* [a party leader of a regional branch of the Nazi Party] or the head of a puppet British Government.'

Guy Liddell wrote, 'Tavistock of course is connected with the British Council for Christian settlement in Europe, which is a mixture of the Link, Nordic League and BUF and a most mischievous body.' It was no wonder therefore that Domvile was under suspicion for attending a gathering of such people.

It was also in February 1940 that the Admiralty was actively considering a prosecution of Domvile for the letters he was writing, seemingly criticising naval activity. It was considered that he was influencing 'public opinion in a manner likely to be prejudicial to the defence of the Realm or the efficient prosecution of the war'. They also wanted to remove him from the naval list and remove any retirement benefits from him. It was felt by the Government that such a path may not be possible but that a charge of 'treasonable activity' might be considered. It was eventually decided not to proceed down either route.

Domvile was also still writing letters that raised concern. In April 1940, he wrote to Olive Baker. In the letter, he refers to a mention of the German propaganda in Parliament as a 'jolly advert'. He went on in the letter to say, 'There's nothing to be done until the general clean-up comes – we have sunk to such depths of degradation and depravity under our Jewish teachers that nothing can surprise me.' He continues to give her information on the wavelength he uses to listen to the German broadcasts and remarks that 'it's grand'. The file shows underlining of this phrase by MI5. In the same month, MI5 also had a report of a 'secret' meeting at the BUF H.Q. which Domvile had attended. He had secretly entered the meeting by a 'specially cleared passage' and was part of a discussion on a 'purity campaign' that he would lead with Pitt-Rivers. The latter was also pro-Nazi and during the war Pitt-Rivers was a supporter of the appeasement of Hitler and wrote to him a personal letter of congratulations on his annexation of the Sudetenland in 1938. Domvile's continued connections with fascists raised further concerns. The Security Service had evidence that Captain Ramsay was planning to have his Right Club members infiltrated into every right wing, Fascist group. He was particularly targeting Domvile's organisation, the Link and Mosley's BUF. Ramsay's belief, as we have seen, was that they should be ready if they had to take over Britain and provide a new government.

On 1 May 1940, when Captain Ramsay was interviewed by a Fascist journalist, he stated 'I should welcome civil war with shots in the streets'. The Security Service surveillance of Ramsay threw up further associations between Domvile and Walter Bernard Laurence, a barrister in the service of the Duke of Bedford, who was a member of the Link and very pro-German. He was actively anti-government because of Churchill's policies on Palestine. There was also a connection between Ramsay and Domvile and Mary Sophie Allen. She was an extreme Fascist, anti-Semitic and a great friend of Germany. She had many German friends and had actually been introduced to Hitler. She was a former militant suffragette and during the Great War she was involved in a volunteer force, Nina Boyle's Women Police Volunteers, as second in command. This became the Women's Police Service and was accepted by the government for the duration of the war.

After the war it, was expected to disband but Sophie Allen assumed command in 1920 and became 'commandant'. The very militaristic uniform was her own design and she wore it, as her standard dress, for the rest of her life. Despite being arrested at one point for wearing it, the government accepted it as 'harmless' and even used her to go to Germany and advise on the policing of soldiers in the Rhine area. The name of the group was changed to Women's Auxiliary Service. She travelled the world in her uniform and was accepted as a representative of the British police, even though she never was. Eventually, she became an embarrassment and the Security Service took a greater interest in her. She publicly admired Hitler and was suspected of spying for Germany during the war but nothing was ever proved. Her Fascist activities with the BUF became more public and extreme. She wrote for *Action*, the BUF's newspaper. Because of her previous militant attitudes, she raised concerns as to what activities she might get up to, in terms of her pro-German stance. Because of this background, the Domviles' association with her brought them further under suspicion. The Security Service's net was closing in on extremists and on 22 May 1940, Captain Ramsay was put into Brixton Prison.

Around the same time, the Domviles had decided to lie low and moved out of their normal residence in Roehampton to go and stay with their Fascist co-worker, Captain Pitt-Rivers, in Devon. Their arrangements were also a cause to concern the authorities. An agent visiting the Roehampton house found the chief maid un-cooperative as to the Domviles' whereabouts until a warrant was produced. She then informed them that she was told not to reveal where they had gone and all mail was to be put in an envelope and addressed to Captain Pitt-Rivers in Devon. The Admiral would subsequently write a testy letter to the War Minister complaining about liberty and freedom.

Information was reaching the Security Service about Domvile speaking in defeatist terms about the war. One report from The Star & Garter Home at Richmond, where Domvile was a governor, was particularly alarming for MI5. Colonel Edward Gowlland, a distinguished retired officer who had served his country with great bravery, earning a DSO and who now was the director of the home, was prepared to testify to a conversation Domvile had had with a resident. In it, the admiral had stated that 'Hitler was going to win the war' but no one was to worry because he would 'bring the Duke of Windsor over as king and everything would be much better than it is now'. This was not an idle throwaway remark. Count Albrecht Bernstorff of the German Embassy had been reported by Bruce Lockhart to Foreign Office officials, speaking in 1937, that 'Germans still believe he [The Duke of Windsor] will come back as a social-equalising King, will inaugurate an English form of Fascism and alliance with Germany'. Domvile was a Royalist and believed in an Empire ruled from England and harboured this dream of an anti-Semitic Empire based on fascist lines. The return of the king as a dictator would have suited him. Indeed, the king admired the Italian leadership under Mussolini and supported the invasion of Abyssinia in 1935.

Bruce Lockhart, a British diplomat, journalist, author, secret agent, in his diary for 1933 records Edward, as Duke, telling Louis Ferdinand of Prussia that 'dictators were very popular these days and that we might want one in England before long'. It must be said that Edward was pro-German and probably anti-Semitic, as were most in his aristocratic class, but he would never have directly supported the treatment of Jews by the Nazis, despite his comments that this was a matter for Germany. Domvile further said that he knew the French were prepared 'to rat on us and make a separate peace'. He also asserted that he had seen the confidential [Peace] terms and that it would be accepted 'sooner than anyone supposed – in fact within the next few days'. He also informed the resident that 'very soon Hitler would be in this country and that would be to the benefit of everyone'.

The Admiralty was also growing in their concerns over the admiral and a report from them called him 'a chief exponent for the Nazis' cause in this country'. They complained about his association with Nazi leaders such as Goebbels and were concerned that he was too close to Oswald Mosely. The publishing of his articles in the German press was giving an impression that the naval authorities were endorsing his views, which were not in the interests of the country. Furthermore, they insisted his connections to Laurie and his book did harm to the British cause. There was a growing clamour for Domvile and his wife to be taken out of circulation.

A 'confidential and private' handwritten note to MI5 sums this up:

'As [Redacted] of Sir Barry Domvile's I read with horror in today's paper that the ex-members of 'The Link' held a secret meeting in London last week. Perhaps you do not realise that despite all Sir Barry

Domvile did for his country in the last war, that he is now entirely under the influence of his German wife (whose mother was British) as all Germans seem to have this strong influence. I hope that in view of the 5th column dangers, that you are having both these people closely watched.' [The writer's underlining]

In early July 1940, the detention of Admiral Domvile was now actively being considered. A full case review was carried out and it concluded that the admiral had a 'fanatical admiration for Germany and the Nazi system'. It was felt that this had 'clouded his judgement'. There was a reluctance to detain him because of his 'distinguished record'. The only thing that was stopping detention was the lack of proof that he was an actual member of BUF. Much less harmful members of this group had already been detained. The review felt there was a considerable amount of evidence that Domvile was acting against the interests of the country but because there was no hard evidence of membership of BUF detention might be a problem for the Home Secretary to consider. However, it was still thought that some grounds could be established that would allow for such detention. On the basis of this report, on 8 July 1940, having been detained under Defence Regulation 18B, Sir Barry was sent to Brixton Prison and Lady Domvile to Holloway. Compton was sent to Latchmere House for interrogation.

Chapter 8

The Cabin Boy's New Berth

'In fact my cell became quite a cabin, and was much admired by various visitors, invited and otherwise.'
    Admiral Sir Barry Domvile 1943 (*From Admiral to Cabin Boy*)

The Admiral's detention, in his mind, had nothing to do with his own activities. Rather it was a plot that he believed was conceived in the *Protocols*. This fictitious book, which we have already noted even in Domvile's day had been discredited, became the background for Domvile to explain what was behind every ill in the world. Indeed, his assertion was that the 18B of the Defence (General) Regulations 1939, was outlined in the *Protocols* and that the Jews were behind his detention. He spoke of a Jew, Abrahams, being involved in his arrest. In fact, he was arrested by Inspector Keeble of Special Branch. MI5 needed an expert to examine some documents in Domvile's home which they thought might be related to Lord Haw-Haw, the German propagandist broadcaster. Some days after the arrest, the BBC's Mark Abrams, who specialised in these broadcasts, was called in to look at the documents and analyse them. He had nothing to do with the arrest or detention of Domvile. In his book, *From Admiral to Cabin Boy*, Domvile displays a great paranoia about Jews and Masons, coining the term 'Judmas' to describe those whose activity was to control the world. He claims copyright for the term, defining it as 'the principal disturbing factor in world politics for many a long day'.

 Domvile believed that his time in Brixton made him fitter and he settled in to his new abode reasonably well. He recounts the arrival at Brixton when he was handed over to the care of the prison services and the inspector who delivered him being given a 'Body Receipt'. From that time on he wrote, 'I became a body, nothing more: presumably I parked my soul outside the gates to await the day of deliverance.' Domvile describes his first accommodation in Brixton, writing:

'My new residence evokes no tender memories: it was semi-detached, a little larger than a telephone call-box and roofed in with wire netting. It was devoid of furnishings, except for a shelf at the inner end, intended to sit upon but barely wide enough to accommodate a well-upholstered posterior.'

How the Admiral had fallen. From the splendour of his well-furnished Roehampton mansion, he now sat in the sparse surroundings of his cell. It was an uncomfortable experience for him, because of the unknown future and the sounds of other prisoners singing and banging on their doors. He took comfort in a couple of 'swigs' from a bottle of whiskey, that he knew he shouldn't have, but which the 'Inspector had not discouraged the idea of the bottle accompanying me on my journey'. Eventually he 'got sick of it' and became a teetotaller in Brixton. He was moved from his reception cell, enduring a bath in carbolic soap, before he was transferred to F Wing. This was an area of Brixton Prison that had been condemned but was reopened to accommodate detained Aliens and 18B internees. The Admiral found it a gloomy place and his cell again Spartan. He would however become more experienced in prison life and learned how to work the system. The hard board he had to sleep on was 'too close to the concrete' and he used the table and chair in the cell to arrange to elevate it from the floor. His watch was taken from him and he found this a great frustration. His daughter therefore became a 'competent smuggler' and a cheap Swiss watch was secreted in the cell and kept out of the grasp of the prison officers during cell searches. He found himself in a strange world of routine which had its rules and regulations that at first caused considerable inconvenience to the prisoners. However, the Admiral would begin to ignore them and found the prison authorities would soon abandon any attempts to enforce the rules. However, there was still the situation of confinement where he was in solitary isolation in his cell for twenty-three hours a day. He also recounts the moment a prison officer entered his room to discover that the prisoner was his former senior commander when he was a petty officer in the Navy. His horror and incredulity was relieved when the Admiral 'quickly disillusioned him and assured him his eyesight was all right: it was only one of his naval deities that was lying shattered at his feet'. So Domvile, the shattered deity, soon was in a very regular routine, which included a twice daily clearing out of 'slops', causing him to title himself 'hereditary pot bearer to the Governor of Brixton Prison'.

F Wing in Brixton separated the detainees into those who had been given a hearing with the advisory committee and those still awaiting their turn. Domvile believed this was to prevent those still waiting from getting any advantage in the 'one-sided contest with the Tribunal'. The experience seems to have been one of minor deprivation; Spartan conditions with a prison cat and bugs, which apparently did not bite him, for company were his lot. There appears to have been some association with his fellow inmates. He particularly was impressed by the Irishmen who had been detained because of the troubles in Ireland. In writing of Cahir Healey, he compares him as an 'eagle' to the 'carrion crows' who were the British politicians. The eagle, as Domvile saw it, flapped his wings against prison bars whilst the carrion crows were free 'to pollute our public life'.

Domvile, although not overjoyed at being incarcerated in Brixton, was thankful that he had not been transferred to Liverpool or the Isle of Man, as many others had been. Even more so, he was relieved he had not been sent to Latchmere House at Ham Common, where he believed 18B prisoners were dealt with by 'Intelligence Officers of Jewish origin'. It was widely held that forms of 'torture' were practiced there to obtain information from fifth columnists. His son Compton had spent some time there. Domvile abided his time awaiting the opportunity to defend himself before the Advisory Committee, certain that he would be released.

Chapter 9

The Admiral's View of Himself

As the Admiral settled into his new berth, he awaited the opportunity to put his case before the Advisory Committee. This committee was set up to advise the Home Secretary by reviewing the detainee's case and to give their view as to whether someone should be detained or released. The Security Service was convinced that the Admiral and his wife were a threat to the country at war but how did the Admiral see himself?

Domvile claimed that he felt detached from the events and was not bitter at his treatment. He had an arrogance about his situation that was demonstrated when he stated that his friends would understand but those who took an opposite view were considered to have done so in ignorance.

> 'Indeed it is an irony of fate that the better the motives for one's actions, the more likely they are to be misjudged by the ignorant and ill-informed.'

He asserted that what was seen as pro-German activity was no more than 'efforts to improve the friendly relations and mutual understanding between the British and German nations'. He was convinced that his detention was trigged by 'two Jewish gentlemen in the House of Commons'. This referred to questions being asked in the House about newspaper reports on his pro-German views. It is not clear who Domvile was referring to as many members asked questions. He held in contempt the politicians who invoked detention and who claimed they were patriotic. He had served his country 'right or wrong' and was the real patriot. Now he had to speak out because he was convinced that 'on this occasion … the course of the ship of state … being navigated by its bemused pilots was unnecessarily hazardous'. It was, he felt, his duty to open the eyes of his fellow countrymen to the dangers. The Admiral as always had a great passion for the British Empire. He saw a Government who, in his mind, threatened it by declaring war. When he looked at the situation he saw that a win, lose or draw in the war created a *'tertius gaudens'* (a rejoicing third party who benefits from the dispute) which would emerge and that it would not be British. His concern was therefore in the interests of the country. He would later claim that he was justified by events.

He had taken a great dislike to Churchill and was further convinced he was being controlled by Judmas. He had experienced him whilst at the Admiralty and was not impressed, seeing Churchill's role in the current situation as not good for the country. In the Great War, Britain had been concerned for the Empire and its navy that secured it against the German naval threat. After the Great War, Domvile believed a different course should have been taken with Germany. The Treaty of Versailles, Domvile considered was naïve and that the idea it could succeed was 'just silly'. He thought that the League of Nations which emerged from the treaty was the work of Judmas. From this the handling of the lands given back to Poland was an error. The handling of the Mandate for Palestine and Balfour's declaration also was fraught with risk, in his opinion. The United States refusing to join the League again showed that the British and American relationship was not good for Britain. Domvile asserted that, as ever, Judmas was behind all this. The whole Jewish influence was using the situation to dominate the world's finances. Not only was the folly of the Government seen in the way they dealt with Germany but their handling of the Irish crisis also showed a lack of wisdom in protecting the Empire. Once again, Judmas was to blame. This conspiracy theory dominated Domvile's world view and he was on a mission to save Britain and the Empire.

He looked at the situation after the Great War and saw the difference between France and Britain as foolish with France occupying the Ruhr to enforce the Treaty and Britain trying to rebuild Germany. He appeared to support France's attitudes yet still believed them to be a weak nation. On Hitler's arrival on the scene the Admiral believed that Jewish influence changed the policy of the Government. This was in the context of Britain's dislike of the German treatment of the Jews under Hitler. He himself did not offer any condemnation of Hitler's actions. He was more concerned about Britain's decision to end the Anglo Japanese Alliance, seeing this as a threat to the Empire. He blamed the United States for this and once more claimed the hand of Judmas was at work. The contrasts in Domvile's world view was seen in his condemnation of Churchill's role in the Washington conference, which Domvile saw as duplicitous, and his approval of the fascist Captain Ramsay's role in using the stolen American papers by Tyler Kent, to expose Churchill's dealings with America. Domvile in fact believed Ramsay should be 'congratulated' for this.

His anger continued against Government policy, seeing money that should have been spent on the Empire being diverted to deal with Germany. He strongly believed that Jewish influence had meant that Germany was not treated justly and that Judmas was benefiting financially by what was happening in Germany and Poland. When he therefore turned to Hitler he shows a great admiration for him. 'This remarkable man was fully alive to the evil potentialities of Judmas and was determined to remove its influence in European affairs.'

The only thing Domvile can see wrong with Hitler's horrendous treatment of the Jews was that it was 'tactless' and made enemies and thus obscured his 'good qualities and real greatness'. He then went on to blame the press who distorted the true picture. Domvile's satirical comments are telling about his views on Hitler:

> 'Of course Hitler came in for the worst of it: Hitler the paper-hanger, Hitler the Rug-biter. I could not help feeling sometimes that if Hitler could produce such striking results on a diet of rugs, our Mr Baldwin might have given a trial to the system, through the medium of the whole carpet stock of Maple's and Hampton's emporia, and even Mr Churchill might have improved by chewing a couple of Persian rugs occasionally.'

It should be noted that the term 'Rug-biter' arose from rumours started in Germany were the term '*teppichfresser*' was used to describe Hitler in a rage, when it was said he would throw himself to the floor and chew the rug. The English press did pick this up without any substantiation of the truth. Hitler chewing carpets would certainly amuse their readers.

Hitler had trebled his army and established an air force, both in contravention of the Versailles treaty. Hitler had also carried out 'Operation Hummingbird', known as 'the night of the long knives', in which he eliminated his opposition. It was in September of 1935 that the notorious

Nuremberg Laws were enacted. These laws were a forewarning of what was to come as they were the first steps to rid Germany and Europe of all Jews and to carry out the Holocaust.

It was also in 1935 that Domvile paid his first visit to Nazi Germany at the Nazis' expense. On this visit, he said he discovered that Judmas and the British press had 'served up to British breakfast tables' a fiction about how evil Germany was. This was a very naïve view. What Domvile does not reveal was that he saw the 'goosestep for the first time' and there were 'lots of Nazi salutes and *Heil Hitlers*. I soon got quite adept'. His diary of the visit also states, 'Hitler, who gave them back self-respect and raised them from the slough of despair.' Domvile also visited the SS and SA troops and on one occasion he was asked to review them and was treated as an important guest. He also met regularly with, and appears to have had a fondness for, the Nazi leader Theodor Eicke. Eicke executed Ernst Rohm in Hitler's purge and Domvile records that Himmler told him Eicke was illegitimate. Himmler protected Eicke and even though he had been imprisoned for bombing political enemies and confined to an asylum, he was appointed as head of Dachau, Hitler's first concentration camp. He was a prime mover in establishing these concentration camps with their rigid and harsh discipline. Domvile also at dinner proposed Hitler's health and at these dinners attended by the SS, he notes their rings and the inscription '30-6-34 the date of the clean up last year!!' [The exclamations are in Domvile's diary entry]. There are obviously a great number of conversations about Anglo/German relationships with Domvile writing, 'Everyone is well primed for an Anglo/German entente'. Throughout his visit, Domvile enters details of meeting many prominent Germans and it becomes clear he is being groomed as a bridge for German propaganda into England. Indeed, he saw himself as a key ambassador for Germany in England. At one point he is 'given a Nazi propagandist book which Pudd will like'. Domvile also notes, with apparent approval, that the Nazis have closed down all Freemasonry museums and stopped all rituals. He particularly enjoys a visit to a museum against Freemasonry and its displays showing 'Jewish and Freemasonry rituals are the same'.

His summation of a visit to Dachau Concentration Camp was that 'they [inmates] had very pleasant work to do, and so on, and the camp was very comfortable and the food was very good'. Anyone who has visited Dachau would be amazed at Domvile's account. The cells contained within them a permanent metal box which was about 2 feet square to the height of the ceiling and in which it was impossible for a human being to sit down. Prisoners were kept in these boxes for days and in extreme cases weeks, without food and water or toilet facilities. It would seem these were never inspected by Domvile. Indeed, Sir Arnold Wilson also visited Dachau at the time and was appalled at what he found. He wrote in *The English Review* June 1934 edition, in relation to the treatment of Jews there, 'things were being done of which no reasonable person could approve … In this matter at present I can see no light'. Stanislav Zámečník, who was a prisoner at Dachau, wrote the history of the camp. In it he described how the camp was prepared for foreigners to present a model prison environment. He wrote,

> 'In the following period [after 1934] a unified, detailed scenario for visits [by foreigners] was worked out and routinely adhered to. Visitors were shown a sort of theatre of the absurd, which many of them saw through, but not all, apparently.'

When the British Legion visited, the prisoners were hidden away in an inaccessible part of the camp and German guards played the role of prisoners. Domvile was either naïve or deliberately obtuse and either saw what he wanted to see or really was deceived by his hosts. Whatever the case, he returned from Germany convinced that if war were to break out, Britain would be confronted 'by the formidable combination of Germany, Italy and Japan'. In this he was anxious to encourage a relationship with Germany, believing that Britain should concentrate on the Empire and leave Europe to its own devices. He argued strongly that if Britain entered into conflict with Germany, it could not in turn deal with an aggressive Japan. Britain had failed to deal with a weak Germany and now it was strong the situation was more difficult. He therefore felt that politicians who 'got involved with Europe were stupid'. They should, he argued, establish a firm alliance with Germany and leave Eastern Europe to be sorted out between Russia and Germany. Any other approach was part of the Judmas conspiracy. The Admiral concluded, 'I could only try and point out to my countrymen the strategic danger they were running so needlessly, by pursuit of a faulty foreign policy.'

One way Domvile went about pointing out 'the strategic danger' was to tour the country with a series of lectures. One such lecture was at Chatham House in 1938, where he lectured the great and the good of the military world, on his belief that Germany was 'the most important country to be at peace with'. He argued that, '… they [the government] had completely thrown overboard the sound principles upon which our Empire had been built up and successfully defended.'

He also railed against the sacrificing of the Anglo Japanese alliance. Again it was all down to the underlying influence of Judmas. From such lectures he came away with the idea of an organisation that would actively promote the German-British relationship. He spurned the AGF which was in existence (because it was 'patronised by Judmas) and established the Link as we have noted above. He appeared to welcome 'Hitler's New Order', and lambasted his opponents who opposed it. Particularly 'the Jews and official Labour'. He claimed his work was an uphill struggle because of 'the constant output of vituperation and falsehood' appearing in the national press. He argued that their representation of Germany was nothing like the truth and in 1938 he welcomed the Munich Agreement as a setback for 'warmongers'. He truly believed that appeasement of Hitler was the way forward and that any guarantees to Poland were 'a dud cheque' that could never be honoured. Poland, he argued was in 'possession of stolen land' [from Germany] and they should accept the reasonable demands being made on them by Germany. His efforts to persuade his fellow countrymen to accept similar views to his own through the Link, was met with 'Jews attacking us from every possible angle'. He battled against this because he believed that Anglo-German friendship was the key to peace in the world. In all of this Domvile did really see himself as the crusading knight, fighting for the old ideas of Empire. He was desperate to preserve this old order of the superior British Whiteman, who knew what was best for the rest of the world.

The outbreak of the war put an end to the Link and was a great disappointment to Domvile. He felt that, 'The intense enthusiasm of the German people for the Nazi regime, and the hopes thereby engendered in German bosoms of achieving their rightful position in the world were given little credence in this country.'

He dismissed the reports of 'the naturally biased refugees [Jews] from the Reich' that was informing public opinion. Domvile appears to have had a confusing mind set on Jews. On one hand he claimed not to blame all Jews yet writes, 'I do not blame the Jews, except so far as their aims are inhuman.'

The Security Service notes indicate a similar view, seeing the Admiral as confused and a 'bit of a fool'. He also suggested Russia was a front for Jewish influence, which flies in the face of history, with the number of pogroms that were carried out even up to 1906. He also asserted that every revolution involving national movements was also the work of Jews and Masons. Domvile saw Hitler as challenging Judmas and was grieved that Britain should go to war with him. He compared himself to Herbert Morrison who had been opposed to the Great War but who, unlike him, had not been sent to jail. He did not disguise his contempt for Morrison who now was a supporter of war against Germany. An amusing insight into the Admiral's mind comes when we compare his many references of admiration for Hitler and his attitude to Jews and his thoughts about his jailers, when he refers to them as 'little Hitlers'.

Domvile continually challenged Churchill's policy towards Germany, making his views clear when writing, 'Was it sound policy to set alight the British Empire House, in order to have the satisfaction of roasting the German pig? Was the little bill in blood and treasure justified?' He believed the politicians had no mandate to go to war with Germany. He once more saw the influence of Judmas:

'The present war was brought about by Hitler's challenge to Judmas; he was the first man since Napoleon, with the courage to tackle it openly. His new economic and financial plans for Europe struck at the very roots of Judmas policy.'

Writing of Judmas as a 'canker eating out the heart of England', he spoke of the next war and though he expected not to be here for it, he wanted to make a start on 'a clean new England' before he went. This had echoes of Hitler's desire to have a clean new Germany through the Nuremberg Laws and the cleaning of the German blood line. Indeed, the Admiral wrote:

'This [immigration] had led in course of time to a generous admixture of various stocks in our national blood, and has presented on particular difficulties, except in the case of the Jews, who are a category by themselves.'

He discussed the idea of sending the Jews to their own homeland, and recommended that should be Eastern Siberia. He also objected to Jews being able to change their names to English names, seeing it as a means for the secret infiltration of Judmas. He was fully aware of the attacks on Jews in Europe by Hitler and distanced himself from any suggestions that he would advocate any similar actions. His course was one of political and civil means to prevent the Empire being destroyed by the Judmas influence.

From this we can see that Domvile held a deep anti-Jewish/Masonic attitude that he felt was ruining the world. His passion for the Empire led him to believe that Europe was not strategically important to Britain and that it should be left to Russia and Germany to deal with. He had no regard for Churchill who succeeded Chamberlain and argued that his own activities were geared to a peace with Germany and a reinforcement of the Empire. It was this activity however that led to the alarm of the Security Service and Domvile would be given the chance to explain himself to the Advisory Committee.

Chapter 10

The First Appearance before the Committee

It was at the Berystede Hotel in Ascot on Tuesday, 22 October 1940 that the Advisory Committee convened as Court One. The members of the committee were Norman Birkett KC as Chairman, with the Right Honourable Sir George Clerk GCMB, CB, Professor W E Collinson MA, PhD and Sir Arthur Hazlerigg Bt. as his fellow committee members. G.P. Churchill CBE acted as secretary. Birkett was a liberal lawyer and a former member of parliament. He had an exceptional reputation for fairness and was ideal for his role on the committee, which was unpaid as were all members. Clerk was a former diplomat and ambassador to Paris and well connected to the Foreign Office. Collinson was an ideal man to examine Domvile. He was with Naval Intelligence during the Great War and was fluent in German. Hazlerigg was simply an old Etonian who had become involved in public service. He was a Staff Officer in the Great War and that appears to have been his only qualification to serve on the committee. The secretary, Churchill, was a former diplomat and his role was purely to record the activities of the committee and maintain correspondence. One notable point here is that Domvile has a dairy entry for 30 May 1935 that records Birkett meeting and congratulating him after one of his lectures. Yet during the hearing, despite the mention of a court case in which Birkett acted, there is no mention of this other meeting of the two.

The hearing began with Birkett asking Domvile about the application for habeas corpus and whether he wished to postpone the hearing until it was dealt with. The Admiral clarified that he was postponing the application until the committee had reviewed his appeal. The session then proceeded, with the committee confirming the Admiral's details as to birth and naval history. He was then asked to what he was devoting his attention since his retirement from the service. To this he replied that he was enjoying himself and the work in connection with friendship with Germany. The committee then turned to the founding of the Link. Domvile explained that he had been to Germany first in 1935. He had been invited by a friend called de Sager. The committee were interested in why Domvile had become interested in friendship with Germany and to this he replied that it was 'a long story'. The long story began with Domvile explaining his views on the position of Germany, Italy and Japan as possible enemies. Since the Great War he feared that British policy was not going in the right direction in terms of strategy to deal with this. He therefore saw friendship with Germany as 'the key' to redirecting this strategy. To this end, he told the committee, he had founded the Link and became its chairman. When asked if there had been any communications with Germany before the Link was established, Domvile said 'no'. Yet he had just confirmed he had visited German in 1935, two years before it was founded. The Admiral explained that the Link was brought into being so that 'all classes' of people could be involved and understand the German view. He also wanted to see them being able to travel to Germany through exchange trips with Germans. When Birkett asked Domvile if the Link's 'real purpose was to disseminate German propaganda in this country', he reacted with a strong 'that is absolutely untrue'. However, he went on to state that the object of the Link 'was to disseminate a better knowledge of Germany in this country. If that means German propaganda, then I suppose you would call it true'. The Admiral was then asked if the Home Secretary had banned the Link to which Domvile retorted sharply that he had not. He alone had taken the decision to end it on the outbreak of war. Birkett queried whether the Link was a banned or illegal organisation to be told by Domvile that it was not. The Admiral then confirmed that he had spoken at Link meetings over the whole country and that these meetings were always public. Sometimes the local press reported them and sometimes they were ignored. Pressed as to whether any of the meetings were 'private', the Admiral was emphatic that they were all public because they wanted the publicity.

The questioning then turned to Domvile's visits to Germany. He confirmed that he had visited Germany twice after the Link was founded. Asked about meeting Hitler, he said he had met him and shook his hand. He acknowledged that he knew Himmler and had met him previously. As to Goebbels he said had only met him and shook hands with him, however, Domvile's diaries suggest this was not true. Unlike Hitler, Domvile had shared the 'Royal Box' with Goebbels and had been in correspondence with him. He had also met and shook hands with Rudolf Hess but had not met Goering. He had seen the Nazi Julius Streicher but did not meet him. This had all happened at the Nazi Party rallies at Nuremberg. Domvile said he had not had any conversations with the German leaders as they spoke no English and he spoke no German. A question has to be raised here regarding Domvile and the German language. In 1936 when he visited Germany, his diary shows that he visited a number of rallies at which Hitler spoke. On all occasions he appears to understand what Hitler is saying. In one entry he writes, 'It's [Hitler's speech] about the colonies. I wish they had left him alone that will make trouble'. On another speech he writes, 'Hitler spoke very well from the Tribune. His words clear- A most impressive spectacle'. As we will note later on he also makes a diary entry where he says he 'listened to Hitler' on the radio at home in Roehampton. We also know he was good with languages, having won the distinguished prize for French, whilst in the navy. It can only be concluded that Domvile could get by in German and his contacts with German leaders more than he has admitted at the hearings.

Birkett suggested that a number of British people attended these events to which Domvile agreed. He named Lord and Lady Mowbray, Lady Snowden and Lord Allen of Hurtwood. Domvile was pressed further as to any consultations or any German influence on the Link. He was adamant that Germany had none and furthermore, he argued, that they were not particularly keen on it at first. The Admiral confirmed he did not know all the members of the Link as they were scattered over the country. When asked if any of them were anti-British or pro-German, he replied, 'I hope not'.

This line of questioning was continued and the question was asked as to the Admiral's knowledge of any anti-British or pro-Nazi activities at the Link meetings. He then admitted that he had been aware of such activities and he had received some complaints from members about it. He had written back to them with his view that people were invited because of their knowledge of Germany and he could not be responsible for the content of the meetings. The committee were obviously unhappy with this and asked Domvile if he had expressly made clear that he did not approve of the pro-Nazi activity. He appeared reluctant at first to confirm this but eventually he stated that he had actively made his disapproval clear. There is no evidence in any document that this ever happened. When Birkett put to Domvile that one of the reasons for his internment was that the Link was 'believed to be subject to German influence and subject to German control', he reacted angrily. He 'strongly resented' the statement because it caused prejudice and maintained that the use of 'believed' was wrong as the Link was either subject to German influence or it was not and it was not, according to Domvile. Birkett pointed out that the authorities had to use 'believed' because if the Link was subject to German influence, that fact would be kept secret from the public and the authorities.

Domvile's response was that the first time any such allegations were made was by the Home Secretary, Sir Samuel Hoare, in the House of Commons. It was then that Hoare accused the Link of receiving money from Germany and spreading propaganda. Domvile again strongly denied this. He gave the impression of being ignorant of the activities of Carroll who had been receiving money from Germany for 'advertising'. Again there is evidence in his diaries, as we will see, that this may not be true. Birkett again referred to what the Government believed about the Link:

> 'The ostensible object of the organisation [the Link] was a disguise to cover the real purpose of the organisation, viz. the dissemination in Britain of German propaganda.'

Replying, Domvile said he would 'hardly call it propaganda', what the Link did. He reiterated that the Link wanted to 'disseminate in Britain a knowledge of Germany', to encourage people to write letters and to arrange exchange visits between British and German families. Birkett continued his questions asking if Domvile and the Link supported German aspirations to take back the Colonies [given away under Versailles]. Here Domvile was not clear and evaded the question. He stated that the Link 'was not political' but admitted that speakers at meetings did address political issues. He had no doubt that speakers at meetings did support Germany wishing to regain the Colonies, but he again insisted that the Link was non-political. He was then asked about the letter written by Karlowa cited above and if he was aware he had written it. Because of the date (15 December) Domvile assumed it was a Christmas party and dance. Domvile could not remember inviting him, insisting he did not like him. Yet he records in his diaries various meetings being arranged with him, without any comments on liking or disliking him. He does make many comments on others of a negative nature.

Domvile was then questioned again about his trips to Germany and his meetings with Hitler and the Nazi leaders. He was asked about the letter from Walter de Sager, a half Swiss, half German closely connected to the German government. In it, the committee reminded Domvile, he was invited on 26 July 1935 'to meet some of the prominent naval people' and to go on a 'chamois [wild goat] expedition with Himmler'. Domvile confirmed he had gone to Himmler's house and then to the concentration camp at Dachau before going chamois shooting. He had then visited his wife's relatives in Munich.

What Domvile did not mention was that he was on Himmler's New Year card list. (His 1938 diary records that fact). Questioned as to the committee's understanding that Domvile had 'many German friends', he replied that de Sager's approach to him was through Lady Roydes, the widow of a former Rear Admiral, Sir Charles Roydes and not a German 'friend'. This is not quite the true picture. Indeed, Lady Mary Roydes did introduce de Sager to Domvile, but it was to ask him to visit Domvile at home in Roehampton. It was at this very first face to face meeting on 1 July 1935 that de Sager had invited Domvile to 'meet Hitler and other important Germans'. Furthermore, Domvile knew exactly who he was. His diary records 'Walter de Sager – Swiss, but a German propagandist'. On 9 July 1935 Domvile met the German ambassador for dinner and discussed the invitation. The German ambassador 'gave the OK to de Sager' and encouraged Domvile to go to Germany. Domvile again meets up with the German ambassador on 13 July 1935 and hears from de Sager 'suggesting most attractive trip in August'. The formal invitation would follow. This is a pointer to the Germans being keen to get Domvile on board for propagandist purposes as the 'war mumblings' had been started as early as 1934, also noted in Domvile's diary. Furthermore, Domvile continues to meet up with de Sager after his visit to Germany and his diary shows that he met him and his wife on 17 February 1936 for dinner in England after they had been 'scared out of Germany'. A few days later he takes him to meet Nesta Webster 'an interesting woman' who Domvile writes, 'lays down the law too much' and 'we discussed Germany, Jews and other things'. Webster was a member of the BUF and the Link. She was a great believer in conspiracy theories. In 1919, she had published *The French Revolution: a Study in Democracy*. She claimed in that book that the Jews had prepared and carried out the French Revolution as well as being behind a world takeover plan. The committee were unaware of these facts and Domvile did not enlighten them any further.

In this ignorance of the real facts, the Chairman then moved on to the assertion that Domvile was 'sympathetic' to the Nazi regime in Germany. When asked directly if he was sympathetic to the regime his reply was interesting, as a piece of well-crafted equivocation:

'No. I am sympathetic with the idea of friendship with Germany. That is all I am concerned with: whatever their government is, is their own affair: but the particular kind of government I am afraid is not my affair. If they have a Nazi government and it suits them that is their business.'

When pressed as to whether he had ever praised the Nazi system he responded, 'I have often said it had many good points and so it has.' One can only conclude that Domvile considered Nazi Germany was not the anathema that the British Government believed it to be.

This is further confirmed when Domvile makes an unguarded reaction to a question about his visit to the Dachau concentration camp. Asked if he preferred to be in Dachau or Brixton, his quick response was, 'Dachau'. He then retracted this saying that it was unfair 'because I have been very well treated at Brixton'. In other words, he may not be so well treated in Dachau, which puts a different slant on his comments earlier about how wonderful Dachau was. Asked if Jews were the main population at Dachau, Domvile said there were four categories including hardened criminals.

The committee then appears to be a little unprepared for the next area of concern about Domvile. He had written an article for a Berlin newspaper in which the Government claimed he had given the impression that he supported the return of the Colonies to Germany. This, the Government argued, had given the Germans the idea that a high ranking naval officer was reflecting Britain's view on the matter. The problem was that the committee had not seen the article and did not have a copy of it. They asked Domvile if he could give them a copy. He at first said he could not remember the article, yet he remembered that a translation into German was done before it was sent. When asked who confirmed the translation, Domvile replied that it was Carroll. The secret service had underlined this fact as important and the suspicion that Carroll may have manipulated the article. Domvile continues to come across as a bumbling fool who professes he cannot remember anything about the article written three years previously. Was this an act or does this reflect Domvile's real character?

The committee then turned to examine his preface to *The Case for Germany'*. Again, he comes across at worse as a fool or at best totally naïve or perhaps he was simply lying. Put to him, that the book was being used as propaganda by Nazi Germany, he denied knowing that would be the case. He stated he had not read the book and that he had only written 'a little preface'. As we have noted, Domvile was present at a meeting where Laurie launched the book and spoke of it. His final statement on this point was interesting,

> 'It was written for consumption in England. It was written with the object of the whole of the Link, to explain the German case, as Professor Laurie saw it, and my preface merely said that he was one of those who had been working for Anglo-German friendship and I did not pretend to have read the book.'

Bearing in mind that the book was extravagant in praise of Hitler and the Nazi system, he seemed not to appreciate why the government was concerned that a senior retired naval officer should be associated with it.

So what of Domvile's activity with two pre-Nazi organisations, Information and Policy and the British Council for Christian Settlement in Europe? Again, the Admiral appears evasive and unclear in his answers. Yes, he did attend meetings. Yes, he did take subscriptions to their publications. However, no, he was not a member nor was he a 'moving spirit' within them, claiming he refused to 'belong to any political group after the war started'. The committee was interested in his knowledge of Lord Tavistock's secret visit to Dublin to meet a German minister. Once again Domvile acknowledged he knew of it but only after it happened and had attended two meetings to be informed of what had been agreed. The chairman advised Domvile that he was being given every chance to get the record straight, no doubt aware of some of the secret background papers and meetings. He therefore asked Domvile if he knew Captain Ramsay. Again the Admiral draws this out. Yes he did know Ramsay. The questioning went on:

Birkett: Was he a friend of yours?
Domvile: I knew his wife: yes
Birkett: Why I am putting these questions is this: had you anything to do with Ramsay politically?

Domvile: No. Nothing whatever.
Birkett: Nothing whatever. Did you know of the Right Club?
Domvile: No.

The Admiral continued to deny any connection with Ramsay politically although he did admit he met him at meetings. The Chairman indicated he would be returning to these meetings, but did the Admiral know Oswald Mosley? Here the answer was clear, 'I know him very well.'

Although he knew Mosley, Domvile denied being a member of BUF. This was in fact not true; he was a member but the Security Service were unaware of this at the time. Domvile had been writing for *Action*, the BUF's newspaper, under the name Canute. When asked if he sympathised with BUF the Admiral was careful in his response. 'With portions of it, their foreign outlook particularly. I did not know a great deal about … their domestic policy? … their home organisation or policy, but their foreign outlook I did because it corresponded to my own views.'

This portion of Domvile's transcript is heavily underlined by the security service. When asked to put his views into one sentence Domvile replied, 'Non-interference in the affairs of Eastern Europe and greater concentration on the affairs of the British Empire.' He continued to assert he had no 'association' with BUF but yet admitted he had written for their publication *Action*. Domvile fails to indicate that he had a great admiration for Mosley from the start. In a diary entry of 8 July 1935, we find Domvile meeting up with Mosley and other fascists for an unusual 'stag party' noted by Domvile in his diary. It was a visit to a lecture. It was according to Domvile 'a brilliant talk – mostly political'. He also adds 'I sat next to Mosley who is very sincere' and that he 'admired him'. His antipathy towards Churchill is seen in this entry as the talk was given by 'the red-headed Braken', writing that he was 'reputed to be Winston's bastard'.

He was then asked about his knowledge of Mrs Dacre-Fox, another Fascist. The Admiral said he knew her as Mrs Elam and she was no more than a friend of his. He admitted he had visited her flat and she had visited his home but he was not involved politically with her. Asked about his knowledge of her, the Admiral knew she was a Fascist and 'an extreme character'. When pressed as to whether she was anti-British he was adamant; 'certainly not'. The security service was interested in what he added, 'No. I think her outlook on foreign affairs was precisely the same as my own, but I would certainly feel sorry to call them anti-British.'

The chairman then returned to Domvile's links to Oswald Mosley. Was he 'closely associated' with him? The Admiral was again careful to say he would not use that term but 'knew him well'. In relation to Mosley, the committee now turned to another concern of the Government. Did Domvile meet with Mosley and other Fascists to plot a fascist revolution in Britain? It is no surprise to find Domvile is careful in his response. 'I have attended several meetings but not of Fascist leaders, of all sorts of people who had been working in the same good cause as we were working for, and we agreed to go on meeting during the war.'

Notes on the transcript show the Security Service's interest in that reply and the subsequent drawing out of names that attended the meetings: Mosley, Ramsay, Elam, Tavistock, Lymington, Norman Hay and others. These were all Fascists. The Chairman asked Domvile to state clearly the purpose of the meetings.

> 'The purpose was a very simple one. We met, as I say we had all been working in the same direction in time of peace, and we agreed to have these periodical meetings and discuss the situation of the day as it stood, the war situation and so forth, but to say it was in any way co-ordinating Fascist activities with a view to achieving revolution is a most outrageous statement, most outrageous, and I take great exception to it. It was nothing of the kind. Nothing whatever went on at these meetings except just a discussion on the current position of the war.'

As far as the Admiral was concerned these meetings were simply 'tea parties'. He was obviously very angry at the charge and in addressing that anger, the Chairman expressed his understanding at his resentment only to be interrupted by Domvile angrily saying with such a serious charge he should be 'on trial for treason'. His anger was not abated when the questioning turned to the matter of whether he was a danger to public safety. It was suggested that the Admiral was more sympathetic to the Nazi regime than to the British regime, to which he responded that it 'was a scandalous suggestion to make'. The committee chairman pushed him further.

Birkett: Would you welcome the defeat of Hitler?
Domvile: I certainly would …
Birkett: Would you welcome the defeat of Hitler and the Hitler regime?
Domvile: No more than I would welcome the defeat of any other German government. I naturally want to win the war, but, as I say, I am no more concerned with the Nazi regime than any other regime.

This last response is heavily underlined by MI5. Domvile appears to be unable to condemn the Nazi regime outright. The chairman again repeated the same line of questioning, explaining to Domvile the importance of being clear. Domvile, when asked if he wanted peace with Hitler, 'regretted' that that was now not possible. Sir Arthur Hazlerigg asked Domvile about the closure of the Link and why Domvile had continued to associate with Oswald Mosley who had refused to close down his organisation on the outbreak of war. The Admiral did not give a clear response, simply repeating he had closed down the Link. Professor Collinson then pursued the matter of the Link allowing distribution of German leaflets. The Admiral denied all knowledge of any such thing happening. However, MI5 annotated the transcript with a handwritten note that Domvile was aware of certain material being distributed.

There followed some general conversation with Domvile and the committee members about his relationship with Himmler and de Sager, with Domvile repeating his earlier responses. The committee indicated they had exhausted their questions and invited Domvile to ask anything about his situation not covered by the committee. He expressed his anger at the Home Secretary, Sir Samuel Hoare, for his House of Commons remarks about the Link and Domvile being financed by Germany. He was reminded that the committee had no responsibility for the Home Secretary's actions. Clearly, the affair had upset Domvile and he bemoaned the fact that it had led to the press having 'thoroughly enjoyed' it. The idea that the Link had received any money from Germany had 'rankled him very badly'. He expressed concern over hunting guns that the police had taken from his home but again the committee were unable to help. A further concern for Domvile was his son, who he said suffered from sleeping sickness. 'They took him to this

Admiral Domvile.
courtesy of http://www.dumville.org

Prime Minister Chamberlain meeting Hitler in 1938.
© *Bundesarchiv, Bild 183-H1216-0500-002/o.Ang*

Adolf Hitler.
© *Bundesarchiv, Bild 183-H1216-0500-002/o.Ang*

The Beer Hall Putsch conspirators.
© *Bundesarchiv, Bild 146-1977-082-35/Hoffman*

The Treaty of Versailles.

Oswald Mosley and Benito Mussolini 1936, probably taken by an Italian official photographer or an official photographer for the Italian press.

Professor Arthur Pillans Laurie, 1861–1949.
WP:NFCC#4

The Nazis dismantle an Austrian border post, March 1938.
© *Bundesarchiv, Bild 183-H12478/o.Ang*

The flag of British Union (Red background, Blue Circle and white flash).

Captain Ramsay.

Women at work during the First World War, showing Sophie Mary Allen (right).
Q108495, from the collections of the Imperial War Museums. Licensed under Public Domain

William Norman Birkett, Elliott & Fry Ltd.

Statue by Konrad Knoll, Braunau, 1866.

Lady Domvile, C. E. Carroll (left) and Prof. Laurie.

Joachim von Ribbentrop posing with a photograph of Adolf Hitler.
© *Bundesarchiv, Bild 102-18087/Pahl, Georg*

The Right Honourable Sir George Clerk GCMB, CB.

Rear Admiral Beamish MP.

William Joyce (Lord Haw-Haw).

George Ward Price meeting Adolf Hitler.

The Truth About ANTI-SEMITISM

Shocking Case of Anti-Semitism at Margate.

by
Admiral Sir
Barry Domvile

Domvile's book, with a common anti-Jewish caricature swatting a starfish in the shape of a Swastika.

The Duke of Windsor reviewing stormtroopers.
© *Bundesarchiv, Bild 102-17964/Pahl, Georg*

Kristallnacht.
© *Bundesarchiv, Bild 146-1970-083-42/o.Ang*

We Have British Quislings

MR HERBERT MORRISON, Home Secretary, in the House of Commons last night defended his actions under the Defence Regulations as right.

He begged the House not to under-estimate the dangers of Fifth Columnists.

"It is really no good trying to make some sort of heroes of these people.

"These kinds of people are nasty bits of work.

"There is something unpleasant, something nasty, about a man who will take the orders of a foreign Government against the interests of his own country in time of war, and that is the kind of people they were."

Potentially as Bad

Among the British variety were people potentially just as bad as Mr Quisling and the Belgian Rexists.

The House agreed to the renewal of the Emergency Powers (Defence) Act, 1939, for another year.

Opening the debate, Mr Stokes (Lab.—Ipswich) complained that the House never intended that persons should be kept in detention without trial indefinitely.

Mr R. Boothby (U.—Aberdeen E.) said the House was somewhat awed that Mr J. Arthur Rank had been good enough to assure the President of the Board of Trade that at present he did not intend to purchase the whole of the cinema industry.

That method of bargaining between bureaucracy and vested interests was very unsatisfactory in the long run. It was an undesirable trend towards pure bureaucracy.

"I would try Sir Oswald Mosley, and if he was found guilty of treason I would shoot him," said Mr Boothby, "or, failing that, he could do some national work under supervision rather than sitting in prison." He would also have Admiral Sir Barry Domvile and Capt. Ramsay brought before some tribunal.

Newspaper report of Parliament's discussion on Quislings, including Domvile.

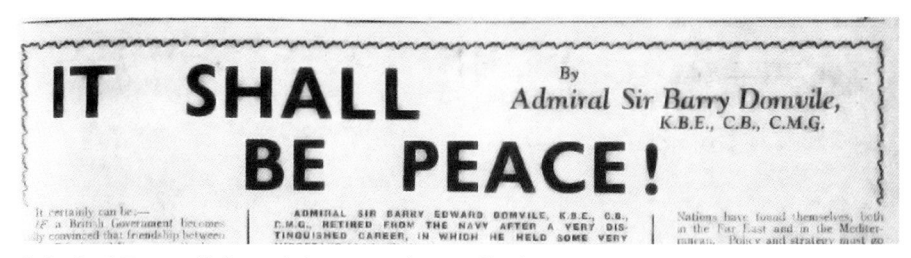

Admiral Domvile's article wrongly predicting peace.

Domvile's book on his detention experience.

Barry Domvile, C. E. Carroll, Raymond Beazley and A. P. Laurie.

Barry Domvile and family, 1932.
© *The National Portrait Gallery, London*

The badge of the International Fascist League clearly shows their pro-Nazism.

The Link badge showing Domvile's intentions of linking Germany to England.

Admiral Domvile and his wife with the photograph of Hitler and a stormtrooper statuette.
© *PA Images, London*

new Gestapo at Ham Common' and he had been held there for four weeks. Domvile was concerned that 'men with hoods' were doing the questioning and suggesting some form of torture was in operation. The committee simply agreed to take a note of the matter, before turning again to Mosley and the idea of a fascist revolution. The Admiral again stressed he had no part in that.

It was interesting when Domvile was asked about how the Admiralty thought of him, he reported that he had had 'good conduct' reports from them. Pushed as to what they thought of him now, he felt there was no change. He was obviously unaware of the letter the Admiralty had sent condemning him. However, he had received a letter from one of his former naval colleagues expressing concern about the Link and German influence which in turn led Domvile to write to the First Lord of the Admiralty, Lord Stanhope, 'strongly resenting' any suggestion that the Link was in any way influenced by Germany.

The discussion moved to the Link's newspaper, the *Anglo-German Review*. Domvile appears to be either deliberately obtuse or truly ignorant of how the paper was financed. He insisted that he paid '£5 a week' and that covered the expenses. He knew of no other financing and accepted the finances were looked after by Carroll. The transcript is again heavily underlined here by the Security Service. They had his diaries and knew that he was not being totally truthful. This ended the hearing and Domvile was informed that other enquires were needed but the committee would do its best to sort the matter out as soon as possible.

Chapter 11

The Security Service Response to Domvile's Hearing

Immediately following the hearing, Birkett was in touch by secret letter to MI5. It appears the committee were persuaded by Domvile that he was innocent of all the charges brought against him. Birkett informed Pilcher, of the Security Service, that the committee were 'extremely disturbed' about the cases against Admiral Domvile and his wife. He felt that 'it is almost impossible that a case has been made out supporting any acts prejudicial [to public safety]'. Birkett's intention was to recommend the release of the Domviles but before issuing the committee's report, he wanted more evidence to support the government's decision to intern them. In the letter, he then gave the committee's opinion on the various allegations against the Admiral and his wife.

In the matter of the Link being under German influence and control, Birkett stated Domvile's anger at the charge and his 'insistence' that it was not true. Domvile had also been 'highly indignant' and had also insisted that 'the Link was not in any manner an organisation used for spreading German propaganda'. It is notable that Pilcher has put a question mark and an exclamation mark against this point. However, Birkett stated he had no evidence to support the claim of German influence and therefore had to conclude the Link was a genuine organisation that 'desired to promote Anglo-German relationships'. The Security Service would have to come up with evidence to support their claims. Birkett then turns to 'a most important point', which was the statement in the House of Commons by Sir Samuel Hoare, that the Link was being funded by Germany. He reported Domvile's intense agitation at these comments and Domvile's assertion that this was 'an untruth'. Again, Birkett wanted evidence for the claim to be given to the committee.

As to Domvile's close links to the Germany leaders, Birkett stated that Domvile had shown this 'to be utterly without foundation'. Whilst accepting that Domvile knew Himmler and had gone shooting with him, this had occurred earlier and before the war. His visits to the Nuremberg rallies had been as part of a larger group from Britain which had also included members of the aristocracy. This again meant that the allegations made had no support in fact. In the matter of the Admiral writing an article for the German newspaper, Birkett asked Pilcher to supply a copy of it to the committee so that they could form their own opinion. Domvile, he wrote, had claimed it was a Christmas goodwill gesture and was 'astonished' that it could be considered as the 'English Naval Authorities in conflict with their Government'. The same situation arose with Domvile's preface to *The Case for Germany*. The committee also wanted a copy of this as Domvile claimed he believed it was for British circulation only. Birkett also reported Domvile's strenuous denials that he was a leading figure in the 'Information and Policy Group' and 'The British Council for Christian Settlement'. As to the allegation that Domvile was involved in the plotting of a Fascist revolution in England, Birkett wrote that he 'particularly resented' the charge and that if it were true he should 'be charged with treason'.

The Admiralty's use of the word 'quisling' in regard to Domvile was then challenged by Birkett. He stated that 'if the Admiralty have some grounds upon which this terse paragraph was based the committee would be glad to see it'. Birkett reviewed the allegation that Domvile was 'pro-German and anti-British and was not to be trusted with his liberty at this time' and made clear his resentment and repudiation of these claims. Birkett stated that Domvile 'desired a British victory in this war'. Pilcher had underlined this and annotated that he 'at first wanted a negotiated peace'. Expressing Domvile's 'being insulted' by the allegations, Birkett wrote that the committee were impressed by 'a sense of his sincerity and honesty'. Turning to MI5's allegation that Domvile might help the Germans if they invaded this country, Birkett wrote that Domvile had repudiated such charges. Pilcher again annotates this part with the handwritten note, 'We suggested that he might collaborate with the Germans after a British defeat'. The whole thrust of Birkett's letter gives the distinct impression that Domvile was a simply bystander to affairs and should be released.

Pilcher immediately brought Birkett's letter to the attention of his colleagues at MI5. These included Sidney H Noakes, Edward Blanchard Stamp (who would both later become judges) and Brian Aikin-Sneath an MI5 agent who was 'the expert' on the Link. In his response to Birkett (which appears to be carefully planned to avoid any immediate action by the committee), Pilcher advised that Aikin-Sneath had broken his leg and steps were being taken to get urgent information from his department for the committee. Furthermore, there were 'about 8 big files on the Link' which would take some time to go through. He pointed out that Domvile was to be viewed in close connection to Carroll, the editor of the *Anglo-German Review* which 'was subsidised through advertisements emanating from Germany'. Pilcher referred Birkett to the Home Office files on Domvile which the committee 'should have before them'. In respect of Domvile's involvement in Fascist activity, Pilcher attached a note of two agents who had been undercover and who had reported on Domvile's involvement in meetings with Mosley and Ramsay. All three had confirmed that Domvile was 'active' in these meetings and not simply a passive attender. One informant in particular, who was the wife of an ex-agent and 'of whose reliability we have no doubt', Pilcher wrote, 'was horrified at the general tenor of their [the Domviles] conversation which was little short of treasonable'. This woman had been present at the Domviles' home on many occasions and was there when a Fascist, Mrs Whinfield, had called to warn the Domviles that Fascists were being rounded up. Pilcher was careful to write very little and ended by suggesting that he arrange for a member of MI5 to come before the committee to give any further information they might need.

It is interesting that at this stage, MI5 seem to feel the need to protect themselves from any charges of their being responsible for Domvile's detention. Oswald Allen Harker, the head of MI5, wrote to Lord Swinton of the Home Security Executive. He enclosed copies of the letters from Birkett and Pilcher which Swinton 'ought to see'. He then twice uses the phrase 'you will remember'. What he wanted Swinton to remember was that it was he who 'wrote a letter to the Home Secretary recommending that orders be made against Barry and Lady Domvile'. He was also to remember that 'the case was really put up by the Admiralty' and that MI5 had only 'sponsored' the detention after this. This gives a great insight to how Harker was always keen to distance MI5 from any mistakes.

However, on 30 October 1940, Noakes of MI5 appeared before the committee to 'assist them with the Domvile case'. The record of this meeting makes it very clear that Noakes, and MI5, were going to control how it went. Birkett outlined the Domvile situation and the committee's view of little or no evidence against him. On the allegation that the Link was under German influence and control, Birkett tried to discover what evidence existed, Noakes took charge.

> 'Before I deal with that, I wonder if you would allow me, I do not wish to get at loggerheads with you and I do not want to state the case too high, and I wonder if you would allow me to make one or two general remarks about what I think is the way to approach this case.'

Birkett was now being led and settled in to Noakes' 'approach'. This approach began with the ignoring of the request for evidence and the MI5 agent agreeing that the Link was started with 'the highest motives', but 'Barry Domvile is a conceited man', he has been described as 'going off'. Furthermore 'Barry Domvile sometimes takes too much to drink'. Having denigrated Domvile's character, the committee, Noakes suggested, should hold anything Domvile said in evidence must be seen in that light. He helpfully added that the way he had put his remarks 'weighed very much in his [Domvile's] favour'. Birkett thought it 'most helpful'.

Noakes pointed the committee to consider the British Council for Christian Settlement in Europe, the pro-German group Domvile had denied having any thing to do with. The committee were asked by Noakes if they knew Luttman-Johnson. They replied that they had and that they knew him to be very pro-German. They also indicated that he was a totally unreliable man. Noakes was obviously pleased to hear the committee's view of Luttman-Johnson as pro-German and indicated that if that was 'the impression in the minds of the committee', he would say no more about who he was. He then proceeded to go through the letters between Luttman-Johnson and Domvile that were referred to above. From these letters, Noakes concluded that Domvile's assertion that he had nothing to do with Christian Settlement was questionable. Had he not been invited to and attended the first meeting of the group when it was established? Were not Gordon-Canning, C E Carroll and other pro-Germans there? Had not Domvile written to Luttman-Johnson stating 'the meeting was a complete success'? Had he not written also that 'The British Council for Christian Settlement in Europe has started'? Noakes thought this was persuasive stuff but Birkett had some doubts. He raised the question of the Duke of Bedford, the Marquis of Tavistock and other prominent figures who had similar views to Domvile. He also noted that Lloyd George himself wanted a negotiated peace with Germany in 1939, in just the same way as Domvile and Christian Settlement. Noakes' response was that the committee had to test the credibility of what Domvile said. Sir Arthur Hazlerigg noted that Domvile 'had rather slipped off the point' when questioned about this matter. Birkett went through Domvile's statement where he confirmed attending the founding meeting but still insisted he had nothing to do with it. Noakes turned to another letter Domvile had written to Luttman-Johnson referred to above, that warned him to be aware of any security agents and the government being 'frightened'. Domvile had also written about Information and Policy, the pro-German paper, and that it 'would have all the details'.

Noakes placed before the committee their options as to Domvile, whilst sowing a seed of doubt. Was he less than candid about his involvement in Christian Settlement and thus raising suspicions as to his real role? Was he really 'the bluff old Admiral who always speaks the truth'?

'We did like him', Birkett responded.

Noakes agreed. 'Yes. In many ways he is obviously a taking personality'

Turning again to Domvile and Christian Settlement, Noakes referred to the letter written by him to Carroll in which Domvile had stated, he was 'always ready to help unofficially. It does them no good if I join because the press call it a disguised Link'.

The discussion continued with Noakes making it clear that the committee had to make up its mind as to Domvile and his pro-German views. However, he steered them to consider the likelihood of the Admiral being ignorant of the pro-German activities at the Link meetings as highly suspect. Furthermore, he went on to stress the very firm connections between the *Anglo-German Review* and the Link. Domvile, he stressed, had written for every issue of that paper, which in turn was edited by the very pro-German Carroll. It was also the case that the *Review* always praised Germany and never once had anything good to say about Britain. Noakes produced copies of the *Review* for the committee to bring home his points.

Birkett noted that in his interviews with Oswald Mosley, he discovered the same thing, with Mosley also praising Hitler but never Britain. There appears to have been agreement with this general point and Noakes reinforced the idea that Link meetings were places that pro-German sympathies were aired. He again brought the pressure on the committee:

'The matter is whether one can believe that Sir Barry Domvile – and it is a matter entirely for your judgment of Sir Barry Domvile – whether you think Sir Barry Domvile can have been ignorant of everything that went on.'

Birkett's response appears to show him being agitated and he pushed Noakes as to how the committee could press Domvile if there was no evidence that he had knowledge of the pro-German activities. Noakes again stated that there was evidence that various speakers had given support to German views at Link meetings but no one had given the British views. There had also been commendations of German public works but again no commendation of those in Britain. Noakes spoke of an agent being present at the meetings, but Birkett argued that this was of no use unless they knew who the agent was and their reliability. Noakes side-stepped this and again reiterated that it was a matter for the committee's judgment as to the Admiral being truthful.

There then followed a review of Germans who had spoken at Link meetings. One in particular had spoken in support of the German concentration camps and this led to an uproar among the audience. There was also a British General Fuller, who had written a book on Fascism and its defence. Domvile's diary shows that he met with General Fuller and his wife as early as the 1930s for dinner on many occasions. In his entry of 3 May 1934, Domvile writes that Fuller is 'working with Mosley'. When the committee wanted to discuss this general, Noakes advised them that 'it is not yet within your purview'. The general had been linked to the *Anglo-German Review* and this led Birkett to state that you could not separate this pro-German paper from the Link when considering the case of Sir Barry Domvile. Noakes had led the committee to the conclusion he had wanted.

Having dealt with what was spoken at Link meetings, the committee turned to written propaganda that was distributed at them. This material was pro-German and anti-Semitic. The committee considered if this was a case of someone having visited Germany and signed a visitor's book and was subsequently sent some of these pamphlets? Noakes made it clear that it was a bulk dispatch and that the Post Office had intercepted a large quantity of material. In fact, Noakes pointed out, the Vice-Chairman of the Link's London branch had written to Ribbentrop's office asking for regular monthly literature. Noakes underlined his point by making it clear that this was what was happening at the Link, even if Domvile claimed he knew nothing about it. Birkett again tried to offer an explanation that it could be seen as the Link wanting to get the official German line. However, Noakes wanted to move on and steered the committee to the 'important matter' of finance. To which Birkett agreed that they should, bearing in mind the Home Secretary's statement in Parliament that the Link had received money from Germany.

Satisfied he had confirmed the close association of the Link with the *Anglo-German Review*, Noakes pointed to Carroll, its editor, having written frequently to the Ribbentrop's bureau for money, ostensibly for advertising. Birkett intervened to state that the paper carried a lot of 'respectable' advertising, some even for British companies. He insisted that there was a difference between legitimate advertising and receiving money 'to support the Link or *Review*'.

'Have you any letters?' Birkett asked.

Noakes answered, 'As I said we have so many volumes of …….'

Birkett's irritation seemed to boil over as he interrupted Noakes. 'Do not burden us with things that are not relevant. We should regard that point as of great importance because of our knowledge.'

There then followed an exchange about what letters would be relevant and just how many people received the *Anglo-German Review*, which was about 5,000.

As Carroll was the main topic of the letters, the committee felt that it would be right to hear Carroll's case before making a decision on Domvile. Noakes agreed that might be a good course and went on to outline the case against Carroll. He had written to the Germans as to the best way to use the *Review* and advertising to influence editorial opinion in Britain.

Here the committee took a break and upon resumption Birkett began to speak, to be immediately interrupted by Noakes.

'Whatever may have been the original idea of Barry Domvile and those who founded the Link in the first instance, it is clear that the Link was, in fact used as an instrument of Nazi propaganda in England.

Its official organ was the *Anglo-German Review* which may best be described as the orthodox exponent of everything Nazi. It is difficult to find throughout its pages any words of criticism of anything Nazi or any praise of anything British, when the latter was not completely in accord with the Nazi model.'

Noakes then went through the activities of Carroll and his contacts with German officials. He outlined the letters from Carroll that clearly had the object of getting the Germans to support the *Review* financially. He quoted Karl Marhau of the German Chamber of Commerce, 'expressing the greatest satisfaction at the way the paper was being run, and he said that it was the first paper brought out by an Englishman which published the truth "in our sense".' He also reminded the committee that Domvile had stated he gave £5 per week for the upkeep of the *Review* and 'did they remember that?' Having obtained the committee's acceptance of that fact, Noakes outlined Carroll's letters to the Germans where he had stated that the *Review* was not financially sound and needed the Germans to assist financially. He had written that their lack of support would 'jeopardise the existence of both the *Review* and the Link'. It was after this that £200 had 'come over'. This, Noakes insisted, was the evidence that supported the Home Secretary's claims that the Link had indeed received money from Germany.

A long discussion ensued around the letters that had passed between Domvile and the Home secretary and the Admiralty and Domvile. It was clear that the Admiralty had concerns about Domvile and after the Home Secretary's statement, had warned him to be careful in his actions. The committee and Noakes pondered why Domvile did not make enquiries of his secretary, Carroll, as to the claims of money from Germany. They also considered the variance in Domvile's statement on the £5 monthly payment to the *Review* and a statement of Carroll that the *Review* made a £5 payment to the Link. There were grounds for further enquiries of Carroll and Domvile.

The conversation then turned to Domvile and his connections to prominent Germans such as Hitler and Goering. Noakes spoke of general reports 'which I do not wish to bring out'. There followed a discussion as to which Nazis Domvile had met. These included Hitler, Hess, Himmler and other minor figures. As to the depth of relationship Domvile had with each of them Noakes posed the idea that one could not fully know but that there were obvious closer relationships with a prominent Nazi Dr Hetzler. Domvile also lived 'within a stone's throw' of a German journalist, Rosel, who had been expelled from Britain. Noakes stated that Domvile 'knew him extremely well'. Noakes again raised the question as to whether this was another case of Domvile being deceived. On that point Noakes suggested that Domvile would have to be examined very carefully.

Then there was also the links Domvile had with other Fascists such as Mosley and Ramsay. The diary of Lady Domvile was then focussed on. In it there was a record of meetings with the BUF and Mosley along with meetings of Information and Policy. There was clear evidence that Domvile knew Mosley very well. In terms of Domvile and Captain Ramsay, Noakes pointed out that a letter from Ramsay's son to a prospective member of the Right Club on 20 July 1939 which stated:

> 'The chief aim of the Club is to co-ordinate the activities of all the patriotic bodies which are striving to free this country from the Jewish domination of in the financial, political, philosophical and cultural spheres. The parties in question are such as the following: The B.U. [BUF], The Nordic League, The National Socialist League, the Link, Liberty restoration League and a few others.'

Noakes indicated that the letter only becomes important when it is considered that Captain Ramsay used a meeting of the central branch of the Link on 16 June 1939 to launch the Right Club. The problem the committee faced was then outlined by Birkett to Noakes. Domvile had admitted knowing Ramsay for some time before the war. He had also acknowledged meetings where he met him. Domvile had called the meetings with Ramsay and Mosley as 'tea parties' and for no political purposes. Domvile had also denied knowing about the Right Club until he arrived in Brixton. Is it possible, he asked, that Domvile was deceived and did know nothing about the Link meeting being used to launch the Right Club? Noakes was noncommittal and again made clear that was for the committee to decide. Then there was the question of other associations Domvile had with Fascists, Olive Baker for example. Domvile had exchanged letters with her which suggested he was promoting the pro-German propaganda station, New British Broadcasting. There was also the matter of Domvile's statements at the Star and Garter home where he had declared 'Hitler is going to win the war'. This was on the testimony of Colonel Gowlland who had given a signed statement of the event. An agent of the Security Service had been present at conversations where Domvile had stated he 'advised Oswald Mosley in everything'.

The committee turned again to *The Case for Germany* and reviewed what had already been discussed before. Laurie had not been detained and neither had a number of leading figures in the Fascist movement whilst smaller fish had been put into Brixton. This led to both the committee and Noakes agreeing there was much confusion over who should be in or out of detention.

The final topic for discussion was Domvile's son who had been held at Ham Common (Latchmere House). This was a former Lunatic Asylum that had been taken over by the Security Service. The committee expressed surprise at their not knowing about it until brought up at another hearing. The committee described the conditions of military guards and reports of prolonged interrogations with suggesting of inhumane treatment. Noakes was bland in his response saying if they were true reports, someone should be held to account.

The hearing with Noakes ended and the committee were left with Noakes' evidence and a large number of items that showed Domvile's views and statements that seemed to suggest he indeed had a case to answer. However, the committee still felt that they needed to recall Domvile to explore the issues raised by Noakes. They were aware the Security files were littered with letters, statements and claims by agents and witnesses along with the complication of other detainees such as Carroll and Mosley which involved Domvile and his activities. One gets the impression that the Security Service had a great deal of material that was open to interpretation, much of which Domvile could not remember or suggested an innocent explanation. It was clear, though, that MI5 wanted Domvile's detention to continue.

Chapter 12

Domvile Re-examined

On 5 November 1940 Domvile was called back to the appeals committee to answer the points raised by Noakes. The committee first turned to the book, *The Case for Germany*. Birkett read out the dedication at the front of the book:

'It is with admiration and gratitude for the great work that he has done for the German people that I dedicate this book to the *Führer*. You have been reading the English side for six years; this book gives the other side.'

'To Hitler we owe the idea of peace pacts. Two nations agree not to go to war for a term of years. This does not involve any alliance against a third Power and this policy was spread over Europe'

Birkett continued, 'Well, you see what Laurie was there saying. "Hitler is a great benefactor because of his peace pacts". Well, now we know what those peace pacts were, do we not?'

This irritated Domvile and his response was pointed. 'Yes, Mr Birkett; are you trying to make me responsible for this book?'

There then followed a sharp exchange of views where Domvile was forced to accept the book was propaganda for Germany when Birkett again quoted the book, 'I thank God that the peace of Europe is in the hands of Hitler', asking Domvile if he could imagine writing that. Domvile struggled to defend himself but his responses showed he knew he was clearly on shaky ground. At one point he declared there was no harm in the preface. However, he did admit that he should have read the book before writing the preface. Birkett was not content that Domvile could see the error in writing the preface and forced the matter on, declaring that Domvile had given the public the impression he had endorsed the book and its contents. Once more he repeated the quote on Hitler and peace in Europe. Domvile was obviously very rattled and retorted, 'It's a long way from that preface to Brixton prison.'

Birkett was very clear on where he stood,

> 'Sir Barry, I have been quite frank with you and I hope you will be quite frank with me. You will forgive me for returning to this, but you are not as other men are, you are an Admiral of the fleet, a director of Naval Intelligence, and you will never divorce yourself from that, and every word you write in the eyes of the German people, or British people, it is Admiral Sir Barry Domvile, late Director of Naval Intelligence in the British Admiralty, you see, and you are there, unwittingly, as you now say, endorsing this man Laurie, you know: "Thank God that the peace of Europe is in the hands of Hitler", in May 1939.'

Domvile was still belligerent and declared he could not be held responsible for the use of the book. Birkett then lectured him on writing prefaces and the need to read the book before writing one. This had no effect on Domvile who still believed the preface was harmless.

Birkett then took a different tack, asking if Domvile knew Laurie well. Domvile accepted he knew Laurie well and when asked if Laurie was pro-German he responded by declaring him pro-British interested in his own country. Birkett was clearly frustrated. Had Domvile not read Laurie's articles in *Action*, the Fascist magazine? Domvile 'didn't think so'. Birkett stated that he could not find words to condemn these articles which were against British interests. Domvile was still not prepared to accept his fault in the matter, arguing that if he had said to someone that 'this is a very good box of matches' and if they then went on 'and lit up a magazine [of ammunition] you would accuse me of being responsible for lighting off the magazine'. When pressed he did not seem to think his Admiralty colleagues would see the book as anything other than the German view. Furthermore, he continued to argue as someone who was promoting German/British relationships, the German point of view should be able to be read by people. As to the fairness of Laurie's book, Domvile argued it was fair 'from the German point of view'. Despite Birkett once more trying to show Laurie as extremely pro-German, Domvile would not accept that argument. Having realised Domvile was never going to move from his positon, Birkett turned to the next matter, the Central London branch of the Link. This was the branch which had entertained pro-German speakers and where pro-German and anti-Semitic literature from Germany was handed out. Domvile denied all knowledge and insisted he had made it clear to branches that no activity of that sort should be conducted. He stated that the Link was non-political. When asked if it was looked on favourably by the Germans, Domvile didn't think it had any special status with them and as long as the Link stayed away from politics, they were happy.

Birkett then turned to Carroll, asking Domvile to confirm he was in at the start of the Link, which he did. The connection between the Link and the *Anglo-German Review* was then agreed with Domvile, with Carroll as the editor of the paper. When it came to financing, Domvile was led by Birkett to state that he had subsidised the finances of the Link, when it moved into the offices of the *Anglo-German Review*, to the tune of £5 per week. When asked if he was aware that Carroll was receiving money from Germany, Domvile believed that the money received was for genuine advertising. Birkett pressed Domvile as to what he knew of Carroll receiving £750 (approx. £45,000 in 2016) from Germany after the Link and the *Review* joined together, which Carroll had stated was 'a gift' and had not been entered into the books. Domvile knew nothing of this which Birkett confirmed agreed with Carroll's evidence to the committee at his appeal hearing, recently held. The committee were also interested in knowing if Domvile was aware that Carroll was discussing with the Ribbentrop Bureau the receiving of 10 marks (approx. £35 2016) for pro-German letters he got published in the British press as a source of income for the *Review*. Again Domvile said he was in the dark on this matter. Birkett then showed Domvile a letter Carroll had written to the Germans that stated the agreement that the Germans would send £200 (approx. £12,000 2016) a month which was needed in part to cover a deficit of £5 in the Link's finances. Domvile expressed great surprise at this and insisted he was never made aware of any deficit by Carroll. He further stated that he had always been shown by Carroll that the books were in order and that there was no deficit. Now that Domvile had seen what Carroll had written, Birkett asked him if he could now understand why Hoare, the Home Secretary had made the statement in the House of Commons. Domvile gave the impression of being shocked by the revelation and now understood Hoare's statement.

Birkett assured Domvile that the committee were prepared to believe he knew nothing of the German finance. As already stated, from the diaries this was probably not true. About the question of Carroll being pro-German, Domvile insisted that he was pro-British and worked twenty-four hours a day 'for the cause'. The committee never explored what 'the cause' meant. As to Carroll's German connections, Domvile confirmed Carroll had married a German wife and did know all the leading Germans but said he had no knowledge of his activities.

The questioning took a turn to discuss what Domvile thought was his relationship with the Admiralty. Domvile recalled that he had been approached by his brother who told him the Admiralty was concerned about German influence on the Link. He had written immediately to Lord Stanhope angrily denying that anyone had influence on the Link and had received an apology in return. Birkett did not take this any further at this time and asked Domvile if he had written to *Truth*, the British Nationalist newspaper. Domvile confirmed he had and was then examined as to whether he had written complaining about Winston Churchill calling the German Navy 'baby-killers'. When challenged why he would do such a thing in a time of war, Domvile could not see the problem. Birkett wanted to know why a retired admiral would not write privately to the First Lord of The Admiralty or even to *The Times*. For what reason would a retired admiral write to a paper that had a reputation of being very critical about the British efforts in the war? Domvile acknowledged that *Truth* was critical and tried to deflect any further questions. However, Birkett pushed on by reminding Domvile that there had been a number of complaints to *Truth* about his letter, complaints that reminded him of the bombing of civilians in Scarborough by the German Navy along with the sinking of the *Lusitania* and hospital ships and lifeboats. Domvile could not remember that, yet, as Birkett reminded him, he had responded with letters against those complaining. Now Domvile admitted 'there had been a long correspondence'. Domvile was keen to move away from this line of enquiry but Birkett reminded him of a particular letter of 19 January when he had 'pooh-poohed' the complaints calling them 'a big song about nothing'.

Domvile continued to avoid the issue and complained of the charge that he had discussed with Oswald Mosley the object of achieving a Fascist revolution. This attempt at diversion was ignored by the committee. Domvile was stubborn in his refusal to see harm in what he had done. He was, he said, 'indignant' by the comments against the German Navy. Birkett reminded him once more of other German Navy actions such as the machine gunning of unarmed fishing trawlers and light ships. Domvile remained belligerent, continuing to argue Churchill was wrong to criticise the German Navy. Birkett once more reminded Domvile he was a retired admiral and his criticisms hurt the Admiralty's efforts. Domvile, Birkett asserted, had in a letter denied any of the German Navy's actions against unarmed craft and thus accused the government of lying. This infuriated Domvile and he argued about the exact wording of the letter, rather than address the point. Domvile now had his memory back and could remember the letter and indeed, he argued, it was a fair letter. To this Birkett read from Domvile's letters where he had referred to the claims against the German Navy and then had written, 'lying is as essential a weapon of war as are guns and ammunition'. Birkett asserted that this was a direct accusation by Domvile that the Government were lying. Domvile responded by saying 'Well, I should not have read that into it myself'.

Birkett's frustration was obvious. He could not understand why a retired admiral and former director of Naval Intelligence would write to a hostile paper and criticise the government and undermine the navy's war effort. Domvile felt that he had the right to criticise the war and that they would have to build bigger prisons to house those who also joined in such criticism. Birkett tried once more to get Domvile to see the difference between criticism of the war and support for the German Navy's atrocities at sea. Domvile was adamant that he had done nothing wrong. Birkett pressed the point that Domvile's actions suggested to the people that the retired admiral was more sympathetic and supportive to the Germans than to the British. Domvile would not accept this and went on about the noble attitudes between enemies and suggesting once again that reports of atrocities may not be true. He suggested that anyone seeking to understand lies and truth in wartime should read *Falsehood in Wartime* by Arthur Ponsonby, published in 1928. This was a book that had given instances of lying by British governments and Naval authorities. One case in particular Domvile was referring to was that of a naval officer who had reported rescuing the occupants of a German U-Boat in the First World War and when he was about to destroy the abandoned vessel, he questioned the U-Boat captain to ensure no one was left on board. The German captain had stated emphatically that the vessel was empty, but it was discovered that four English seamen had been bound and left on board. The U-Boat captain therefore was going to be charged with crimes against the English seamen in wanting their deaths. However, when the matter was raised in parliament, it was soon discovered that the incident had never happened. Domvile was therefore suggesting the charges Churchill was making were also untrue. This of course was not the case as all these atrocities under discussion were fully substantiated.

However, the committee realised Domvile was not going to accept any of their points on this matter and so Birkett asked Domvile if he signed his letters to Germany with '*Heil Hitler*!' Domvile accepted that he had done this but again suggested that it was innocent just like saying 'God save the King'. He argued that whilst staying with a German on a chamois, shoot his host would greet him in the morning with 'God save the King' and he would respond '*Heil Hitler*!'

Sir George Clark of the committee was, with his fellow members, sceptical about this, asking Domvile if this were really true. Clark suggested that Germans used '*Gruss Gott*', as the traditional greeting. Domvile replied 'I don't think so' and went on to insist that his version was correct. His diary for this period in fact does record his version given to the committee.

The hearing then seems to go on a rather rambling journey. Firstly, Birkett returned to the matter of the letters to Olive Baker about the New British Broadcast Service. In a rambling conversation which covered who 'twiddled Domvile's radio', it was suggested that the impression had been given that Domvile was promoting a station that in turn was promoting German propaganda. Once again, Domvile presented himself as an innocent abroad who was involved in a harmless activity that many were involved in. As no progress was made on that subject, Birkett produced a letter dated 3 June 1939 from Carroll, the contents of which was 'rather curious'. This was because he was writing about the finances of the Link and made no mention of it being subsidised by the *Anglo-German Review*. This was not developed and Birkett asked Domvile if his brother had spoken to him about the Admiralty's concerns regarding his connection to the Link. Domvile stated that his brother was 'not very clear' about what Admiral Godfrey, Director of Naval Intelligence had meant. He reiterated his statement that he had written to Lord Stanhope making clear there was no influence on the

Link from Germany. He made clear that he had received an apology from Godfrey and a 'civil letter' from Lord Stanhope. Birkett queried whether or not they had indicated he should be careful, to be told they had not. Birkett, mindful of the letter the Admiralty had written to the Security Service calling the Domviles 'quislings', enquired if Domvile realised a number of the people at the Admiralty might be concerned that someone with his naval record should be running the Link. Domvile responded that if they were they should have told him, but no one did. Domvile's tone must have been sharp, as suggested by Birkett's response. 'I do not know that they were worried; I only asked you.'

This was a strange response as Birkett was aware of the letter from the Admiralty and had even discussed it with Noakes during his interview with the committee. However, Domvile continues to suggest that what he was being accused of in terms of his activity in British/German relationships was something Chamberlain himself would support despite the Home Secretary Hoare's statements in Parliament. This was all 'rather difficult' for Domvile.

Sir George Clerk intervened and reminded Domvile that the chairman had presented evidence that supported the Home Secretary's statement which turned the conversation to Carroll's role in obtaining finance from Germany. Domvile was reminded of the facts of how it was decided not to put the money through the books. He again expressed his shock at the £750 'gift' and stressed he knew nothing about it. Sir George again stated that the Home Secretary's statement was based on this information to which Domvile responded, 'That rather makes your point.' Having got Domvile to this agreement the subject moved to Domvile's view of war.

Sir George asked him if it were true he held that there were 'no rules in war'. Domvile replied there was only one rule, 'the law of expediency'. He believed you could do what you like to 'neutrals and other people'. Furthermore, he was clear there was no use in making rules as nobody else would stick to them. Sir George was leading Domvile to consider his attack on Churchill in *Truth*. If he held this view, then the German atrocities in attacking schoolgirls, sinking hospital ships and attacking the old men of the lightships was acceptable.

Domvile interrupted, exclaiming, 'No, come, no, no, you must not say that.'

Sir George pressed on, 'I just want to get the impression right'.

Domvile then suggested the reports may not be true or perhaps it was a mistake but if a ship was in enemy waters then it is legitimate for it to be torpedoed. However, he insisted, atrocities did not pay. Here, he is not morally against the atrocities, just that they do not pay. They were 'beyond the law of expediency'. Again he was pressed as to whether survivors or innocents should be targeted.

Domvile:	No, good heavens, no!
Birkett:	But they did that.
Domvile:	You make me out as someone very brutal.
Birkett:	That is the reason I do not want to misunderstand you.

Domvile then attempted to clarify his views. He still believed that rules in war were useless because no one would stick to them and atrocities did not pay. 'But regarding war as a thing about which you can make nice pleasant little rules about is absurd.'

Despite having discussed the German atrocities already, when challenged again about his views of them, he strangely asked, 'What are you thinking of particularly?'

Reminded of the confirmed attack on the old men of the lightships, Domvile spoke of how lightships were a legitimate target in time of war. But what about the atrocities? He thought they were disgusting and then asked 'That is absolutely definite?' Being told it was, Domvile still appears reluctant to accept the German authorities were involved. 'I cannot understand anyone doing that. I should think they should be very angry when they got home to think they had done it. I should not think those are their instructions.'

Birkett then lectured Domvile on the 'young Nazis' who had been let loose in this war. They had been eaten up with fervour and adoration for the *Führer*. They 'do not consider any humanitarian rules of warfare.'

'He has no decent feelings at all?' Domvile enquired.

'I do not think so,' was Birkett's response.

Domvile appears to have been much chastened by this questioning on the German atrocities and Birkett once again turns to finance. The matter of the £750 was covered again but this time Birkett indicated that it had been paid in two stages through the Embassy. At this, Domvile's memory came back and he now remembered the payments coming through the Embassy and he thought 'rather funny'. He thought the Embassy was being used to get money in and out at a difficult time. Perhaps Domvile's memory was catching up with his diary entry.

The committee did not take that response any further and asked about the British Council for Christian Settlement. Domvile acknowledged that he had attended a few meetings and the organisers had put his name on a manifesto, but he had them withdraw it and he did not sign it. He confirmed he had been in sympathy with some of their aims. The committee then went through a number of prominent Fascists and pro-Germans; Mosley, Luttman-Johnson Pitt-Rivers, Gordon-Canning, Newham of *Truth* among others. Domvile was happy to call all of them friends and he argued they were all loyal Englishmen. In fact, these people were regular dining companions of Domvile. His diaries note the various meetings and in one entry on 2 December 1937, Domvile writes of a lunch with Mosley and Gordon-Canning and describes Gordon-Canning as 'an attractive man', adding of the meeting, 'I enjoyed it'.

Birkett asked Domvile about the distribution of German propaganda through the Link. He wanted to know if Domvile was aware that a secretary for the Link, Olga Thomas, had written to Heinrich Hoffman in Germany confirming the safe arrival of German literature for distribution to members. Hoffman worked for the Nazis and was Hitler's personal photographer and involved in promoting the Nazi party. Domvile stated he knew about it. Then in the next sentence he said, 'I would like to say I knew about it and I would not like to say I did not know about it.' He explained this confusion by saying he knew the literature had been obtained but did not know it was being sent to members. He acknowledged that Thomas might 'have slipped one in' when writing to a member but he did not pay any attention to it. When presented with a letter written to Hoffman in Germany (in 1937) by an armed forces member confirming he had received a copy of *News from Germany* from the Link, Domvile was 'quite prepared to believe that'. However, he insisted that the Link's official policy was not to get involved in these matters. Asked if he thought Germany was taking advantage of the Link and of him, Domvile replied that they might have done but not with his cooperation.

The matter now turned to the question of whether Domvile thought Hitler was a trustworthy man. He would not give a direct answer simply saying 'he had done some odd things'. Domvile suspected the motive for the question and was reassured that the committee were only asking for his own benefit, to clarify his position of only trying to foster Anglo-German friendship. Birkett pushed the matter by questioning if Domvile had given the 'impression that you were more favourable to Germany than you were to this country'. An emphatic 'Oh no!' was his response. Then Birkett once again asked if Domvile would be surprised to be called 'a quisling' by his Admiralty colleagues. This time Domvile accepted some may think like that. Then, Birkett wanted to know, was Domvile surprised at being arrested? Domvile replied that he was surprised and when in Brixton expected to be charged with some major offence. Birkett then referred to a letter Domvile had written to Carroll, in which he had written, 'I think we may meet in prison'. Domvile's explanation of this was that after a House of Commons statement on Captain Ramsay, he was aware that some were calling for Ramsay's arrest and that of his associates of which he was one. The conversation then drifted into a brief reference to an article that Domvile had written recommending the return of the colonies to Germany. There was some confusion about the article as no one had a copy and Domvile argued that there were many, even in Government, who thought the same as he did on the matter. This ended the hearing with Domvile accepting the committee was not responsible for his detention.

Chapter 13

Further Hearings for Domvile

Behind the scenes, Domvile's solicitors and others were lobbying very widely for him to have another hearing. The Home Secretary was of the opinion this was unnecessary and refused, referring the matter to the committee itself. However, the lobbying continued and eventually on 31 March 1942, Domvile was called again to attend an Advisory Committee hearing, this time under the chairmanship of John Morris, a Welsh lawyer. In his account of this time in his book, Domvile does not mention this hearing. The hearing got off to a difficult start with Morris saying they would cover the same material as before and Domvile expressing the view that it would be of no use. If the committee were to simply go over the same ground that would mean that the government did not believe him the first time. He then reminded the committee of a recent statement in the House of Commons by the Home Secretary, saying that the Advisory Committee would not cross examine but was only there to hear appellants. He wanted to know if the practice had changed. If they were to continue to ask him questions he stated, 'I will not get any further.' Morris tried to defend the committee by telling Domvile that the Home secretary decides these matters and they were trying to hear his case.

'That is my grievance,' Domvile replied and asked, 'Do you wish to ask me questions, or shall I make a short statement first?'

Morris allowed Domvile to make his statement, which had obviously been well prepared with accompanying papers. Domvile spoke of his detention and initial hearings that led to his continual detention. He had intended to have a case of habeas corpus raised in the courts, but two previous cases that went to the House of Lords showed that this route was fruitless as 18B simply needed the signature of the Home Secretary. He therefore suspended his action. The Treasury solicitor, Valentine Holmes, had made a statement to the court, to the effect that Domvile had withdrawn the writ after he had seen the charges against him. This give the impression, according to

Domvile, that the charges were so bad he did not want them aired in the open. Domvile felt this was very unfair, even though he accepted that his solicitor's letters to the court were ambiguous and open to misinterpretation. Indeed, Domvile declared it 'disgraceful'.

He informed the committee that he now felt 'stuck' and resigned to his situation. When, in November 1941, Herbert Morrison, the Home Secretary, made a statement on 18B detainees, in Parliament. Domvile was enraged and read out the passage concerned to the committee:

'I take the last and smallest group, concerned with acts prejudicial, the number now detained is seventy-one, fourteen of these are members of the Irish Republican Army or associated with it; others are persons whom we believe have been concerned with acts of sabotage, attempts to get secret information, seeking to make contact with the enemy contrary to the interests and security of the State and there are cases about which it would not be wise of me or of anybody else to talk in detail or in public.'

Domvile suggested that the committee would understand that this statement would be taken to refer to him being involved in such activities. He therefore immediately asked for a hearing but was refused as he was told it would not show anything new. He told the committee that he was then visited by Admiral Tufton Beamish, also an MP, who wanted to help him. He would put a question in the House of Commons about the matter. This led to the Home Secretary clarifying his comments, stating he had just given a general picture of the possible reasons for detention. The Home Secretary claimed that people who misinterpreted him did not understand the use and meaning of language. Domvile insisted that if the Home Secretary made such a definite statement, it was he who had not understood the use of language. Beamish had decided to raise the matter again but he had been approached by a number of people to forget Domvile, as he had 'something very serious' against him. There had been, in Domvile's opinion, further incidents that suggested a conspiracy against him, with obstacles being placed in Beamish's way. It was therefore Beamish's request that the committee let him come and speak to them to defend Domvile. MI5's records do show some substance to this claim. Beamish relied on three directorships to supplement his income.

He had been approached and threatened that these would be removed if he continued his support of Domvile. He ignored these threats and continued his lobby on behalf of Domvile. On 19 February 1942 he asked the Home Secretary in Parliament:

'... whether Admiral Sir Barry Domvile, who has been imprisoned for 19 months, is detained under the Acts Prejudicial Section of the Defence Regulations; and whether he will allow this officer, who has rendered 44 years of distinguished service to the country, an opportunity to prove his innocence of acts of sabotage, attempts to get secret information, and seeking to make contact with the enemy, particulars in support of which have never been furnished to him or the Advisory Committee?

'Mr H. Morrison – Particulars of the reasons for which a detention order was made against Admiral Sir Barry Domvile were communicated to him by the Chairman of the Advisory Committee, and he was given every opportunity at the hearing of his case before the Committee to deal with all the matters alleged against him. In the Debate on 26 November on Regulation 18B I gave a general account of the main types of cases where detention orders have been made against 1,886 persons believed to have been concerned in acts prejudicial to the public safety or the defence of the realm, and I gather that my hon. and gallant Friend is suggesting that if any person is detained on the ground of acts prejudicial, his acts can only be of the types mentioned in this general account. This was not of course my meaning and I was not attempting to give an exhaustive summary of every type of act which may be the basis of a detention order under this provision.

'Rear-Admiral Beamish – Is the right hon. Gentleman aware that I had two long talks with this elderly officer and that, judged by every unbiased standard, he now appears to be treated most unjustly? May I beg the right hon. Gentleman to give an opportunity to this officer to reopen his case and make his innocence clear? Does the right hon. Gentleman really suggest that this officer is a danger to the State?'

The MI5 note states that because of this intervention, Domvile was 'rushed before the committee'. Domvile continued to describe the suspected conspiracy and then demanded of the committee, 'If you have anything against me, for God's sake say it but do not go about with this whispering campaign, saying we know something that does not exist.'

Beamish had reported to Domvile a conversation with the Home Secretary in which he said, 'you do not know how naughty he [Domvile] has been?'

Domvile insisted that all the allegations were untrue, yet the Home Secretary was refusing to release him and putting the worst interpretation on the facts. He therefore asked the committee to help him to 'know in what respect I failed to carry conviction to the [previous] committee.' He then invited them to question him.

Morris began by confirming Domvile's career in the Royal Navy, getting Domvile's agreement that he had got the details right. In turning to the foundation of the Link, he asked for a 'sentence or two' from Domvile. Domvile could not just use a sentence or two and insisted on a much longer background to the Link's foundation. With this he outlined a grand overview of his reasons for founding the Link.

He explained his grand view of the Empire, particularly the Anglo-Japanese alliance. In his view, the American insistence on breaking the relationship with Japan was a disaster and he knew it would lead to disaster. He had become alarmed at Government policy with issues in Italy and then Germany. He foresaw that there would be a war that would involve Britain against both Japan and Germany and that this would put the Empire at risk. He therefore believed that friendship with Germany was the solution. He then had embarked on a series of lectures across the country to promote his views. The committee were given copies of a particular lecture at Chatham House, which Domvile claimed had received a great deal of support although the First Lord of the Admiralty did not agree with him. Domvile also gave a copy of his book *Look To Your Moat* to the committee, which he said gave his views on his vision for avoiding the Japanese/German conflict with Britain. The title of the book was from an article in March 24 1916 printed as a 'Candid Review' in the Western Mail. The article gave the 'Doctrine of the sea' which reviewed the dominance of the British naval power and the need to maintain it. Domvile's book was issued without a date but appeared around 1937.

He told the committee that as he looked at how relationships with Germany were being portrayed in the papers and a growing lack of knowledge of

Germans and their life, he believed that something needed to be done. He began to look for ways for British people to visit Germany and Germans to visit England. He wanted to encourage correspondence between the peoples of the two countries:

> 'In fact, we were doing our best generally to give the knowledge and understanding between the British and German people, which was our idea but as it was not the idea of many people in this country we at once found ourselves being obstructed and our efforts being misinterpreted, which I suppose was bound to happen.'

The whole thrust of Domvile's reasons for founding an organisation to promote friendship with Germany, were rooted in this concern for the Empire. In giving the documents to the committee, he thought it would not do much good, even though much of what he had said and written had come true. In retelling Sir Samuel Hoare's 'attack' on the Link in parliament, he declared it rubbish and that the Link members were English men who were trying to establish good relations with Germany and thus by necessity they had to meet German officials but it was always on matters of the Link and never politics.

The rest of the hearing appeared to take on a more adversarial tone with the committee putting very direct questions to Domvile and his sharp responses. In general, the material covered was much the same as previous hearings. Domvile's answers to the many questions were to defend his views as harmless and to be innocent of all allegations. On many issues of controversial letters, Domvile either could not remember writing them or could not remember what he had meant when he wrote them. The letter to Olive Baker regarding Lord Haw-Haw's broadcasts with Domvile calling them 'grand' and underling that word, was a point of long argument. In the same letter, his reporting Ramsay's mentioning these broadcasts in Parliament and Domvile calling this 'a good advertisement' brought sharp exchanges. Domvile's opinion was that he was a misunderstood man who only wanted the best for his country.

One letter in particular became a major focus for the committee. Noakes of MI5 had written to the committee's secretary giving her a copy of a letter that had turned up since Domvile's last hearing. It had been found in the possessions of another detainee, Kenneth Duffield. The letter, referred to earlier, raised great concerns with MI5 and Noakes quoted the particular sentence, 'I work in close touch with Sir Oswald Mosley – just waiting events.' The letter in full helps to appreciate the concerns:

28 Jan 40

'Dear Mr. Duffield

'Thank you very much for your letter – it is nice to hear from old members of the Link – we were beaten by the war – but we shall win all right in the end, even if we have to go through a bad time first. I see from the remarks in your letter that you understand the whole wicket racket and know whose evil influence is behind it. I work in close touch with Sir Oswald Mosley – just awaiting events – I do not know how long it will take to reach the crisis – I do not think anyone does. I heard from Lord Redesdale yesterday – poor man, he has a bad time with the gutter Press – I am afraid his girl is pretty bad – but they hope for the best. I see the Press today have got hold of her address again – and will no doubt try to excavate some more excremental 'news'. Lord R. says they are trying to finish him.

'Well, good luck to you. I hope when the war is over, the Link will once more flourish,

Yours sincerely,
(Signed) Admiral Domvile'

Kenneth Duffield was born in 1909 (possibly in Sweden and became a naturalised British citizen) and was a film screenplay writer who had worked in Berlin. He ran a German translation service from the address in the letter. He was a Blackshirt in Mosley's fascist BUF and an extreme supporter of the Nazis. He was interned under 18B.

The phrases that the committee were keen to explore were: we were beaten by the war; we shall win all right in the end; the whole wicket racket; and know whose evil influence is behind it; I work in close touch with Sir Oswald Mosley; I do not know how long it will take to reach the crisis; I hope when the war is over, the Link will once more flourish.

The first thing Domvile insisted on that he did not know Duffield. He had no memory whatsoever of the person. He had no recollection of ever writing such a letter. He insisted he would never write such things to 'a stranger'. He doubted the letter's authenticity, asking to see a copy of it. On reading the contents he expressed disbelief and still had no recollection of Duffield or the letter. Pressed on the phrases and their meanings, he could not give any idea as to these. He could not explain the 'we' who were beaten by the war or who it was that 'shall win all right in the end'. There was no explanation as to 'the wicket racket' nor who was 'the evil influence' behind it. What he had possibly meant by being in 'close touch with Sir Oswald Mosley' may just be an expression of being his friend? He also had no idea what 'the crisis' referred to, maybe he meant the war. As to the Link's future, he would hope that after the war reconciliation with Germany would be possible and the Link may have a role. All of these responses were in the context of Domvile still not fully accepting he wrote the letter. Members of the committee expressed incredulity that Domvile could not remember the person, writing the letter or the details of such phrases. What the committee did not know was that Duffield was a contributor to *Action* and the *BUF Quarterly*, also a BUF publication. His articles appeared alongside Professor Laurie's in that paper. *Action* itself carried adverts for the *BUF Quarterly* with Professor Laurie's name in large bold type and the list of contributors, including Duffield. As Domvile was a regular reader and contributor to these papers, is it conceivable that Domvile did not know him or at least who he was? There being no acceptance or explanation of the letter, the committee moved on to discuss other letters that had already been covered in previous hearings.

Once again the response was the same from Domvile; lack of memory of events, no understanding why such and such a phrase was used or what he meant. Overriding all this was Domvile's continued insistence that everything he did, wrote or said was all innocent and was being misinterpreted. The hearing ended and immediately behind the scenes there were questions raised by Domvile's solicitors that he did not get a fair hearing. To this end he was recalled to another hearing a fortnight later on 15 April 1942.

This hearing was presented by Morris as an opportunity for Domvile to be given copies of about twelve letters and the intention was for the committee and Domvile to go through them chronologically.

They covered much of the ground already discussed in previous hearings, but the committee stopped at key points to invite Domvile to explain. On certain points, Domvile gave his explanation in terms of innocent and harmless comments on world events. His views were always related to the welfare of the Empire. However, the issues that were raised which troubled the committee did not get much help from Domvile.

In the first letter he referred to his 'ignorant countrymen'. In trying to understand what Domvile meant, he was being illusive, saying he could not quite remember its usage but that he probably meant that people in England were very ignorant of foreign affairs. When asked about a statement regarding pro-German groups written after the war started, that 'we should rope them in' and that 'we should centralise them', Domvile again gave a confused response, not being sure what he meant.

When he had written that he was having 'interesting negotiations with Oswald Mosley and Norman Hay' he could not remember what these were or what he meant. The committee linked this to another phrase he had written in the next letter, 'our plans are maturing well'. The committee wanted to know if the 'negotiations' were linked to 'our plans'. Once more there was a brick wall, Domvile did not know what he meant and even asked the committee to help him know what he was doing at that time of writing.

The committee then tried to dig deeper into his writing, 'hard luck stories of lying Jews'. He repeated again that this was in relation to his visit to Dachau where he found everything was great and yet Jews were reporting crimes against them were happening at Dachau. He did not believe these stories and he imagined that was what he meant. Then there were two pieces of two different letters that the committee wanted to clear up. Why had he written, 'I think soon things may move' and 'I am satisfied with the ways things are going'? The response was consistent; he could not remember what he was writing about. In a subsequent letter he had written about C.E. Carroll, 'I think he is a patriotic and clear thinking man and has some good proposals.' He could not help the committee to understand what these proposals were. Then, there was the 'depths of degradation and depravity under our Jewish teachers', since the last hearing had he any further explanation? This time he remembered writing it but dismissed it as him having 'a bad day'.

Morris returned to the Duffield letter and wanted to consider if the letter was linked to negotiations with Mosley or the plans referred to in previous letters. Was it connected to the allegation of 'Fascist revolution'? There was no further help here for the committee. Duffield and the letter was still a mystery to Domvile. The committee then questioned him about being at a meeting with Oswald Mosley where 'a fascist revolution' was discussed. He only attended for tea and it was not discussed. When pressed, he acknowledged it may have been, but he did not hear it because he is deaf. The final letter was about his stating, 'things I cannot put in writing'. When asked to explain these 'things' he was not sure what they were but perhaps they might be about the Duke of Bedford and peace plans. He told the committee that the Duke had told him of peace talks about Germany that he was involved with and Domvile felt he could not write about them in an open letter. Subsequent questioning would suggest this explanation was not totally accepted by the committee.

This hearing does not seemed to have moved Domvile's situation on and he was again returned to Brixton where he remained. This was despite the fact that the committee did report that they felt he was not a danger and would not act against the country's interests. The Security Service however took a different view and extensive memos from them show that they believed nothing had changed with Domvile. Their argument was summed up in one letter as *'ex pede Hurculem'* meaning that they felt if there was even one part of the whole 'evidence' that suggested he should be detained, that was enough. Their considered opinion was that if he was 'a danger in 1940 he is still a danger today'.

Domvile gives his account of his time, following these hearings, in Brixton. The days are filled with the routines of prison life. Domvile would play cat and mouse with his jailers, having things that were banned and which he would refuse to yield and eventually those in charge would simply ignore them. Domvile made himself comfortable getting to know some of the many people who passed through Brixton, including debtors and cat burglars. Time was spent reflecting on those who had arranged for his stay in Brixton and his account makes clear that his belief was that Judmas was behind every woe that had happened to him.

In December 1942, Domvile decided to write a letter to MPs on the subject of 18B and the detention of people like himself. He had tried to send a copy to *The Times* but this was intercepted and did not reach them. He wrote of those who 'prate of freedom' and who 'practice simultaneously the worst form of tyranny in our history'. He argued that MPs were misled by those Crown lawyers who had drafted the regulations. The 'victims were not protected' but he went on 'they were at the mercy of one man – the Home Secretary'. He decried 'the veiled secrecy so carefully drawn over the Advisory Committee'. He criticised the use of the war being used to prevent the public knowing 'the truth'. He then listed all the things he saw wrong with the committee. These included the vagueness of the allegations, no charges being made, no legal representation, no record of the meeting given to the prisoner and the MPs who enquire on a case are shown material which they then cannot divulge to anyone. He gave an example of a hearing illustrating his points before setting out his remedy for each defect as he saw them.

One MP, John McGovern, on receiving the letter took the matter up with Herbert Morrison. To Domvile's joy the decision was made to release him on 30 July 1943.

Domvile expresses his thanks to McGovern in his book *From Admiral To Cabin Boy* and adds that he [McGovern] was 'a thorn in the side of Judmas'. The book, published when the war ended, rails against politicians and urging them not to be trusted. He ended the book with an interesting statement:

> 'The present war was brought about by Hitler's challenge to Judmas; he was the first man since Napoleon, with the courage to tackle it openly.'

Does this help explain the evasive answers given by Domvile at his hearings? Was he part of a plot to challenge Judmas in Britain?

Chapter 14

Admiral Domvile after His Release

Domvile's release was not met with any great enthusiasm by the British press. His previous pro-German activity and his visits to Germany to meet Himmler and being 'a guest of Hitler' were revived in papers such as the *Daily Mirror* on 31 July 1943. The Security Service were still keeping a watch on him, through agents and mail interception. His release was welcomed by the far Right and an intercepted letter from Captain Ramsay commented that 'the Jew-grip must be being weakened'. Domvile remained in touch with Carroll and Gordon-Canning. He also continued to stay in contact with Mosley and often met him after his own release. The MI5 files have notes on the various occasions they met.

The Security Service's notes show that they had concluded that whilst Domvile may have started out as an innocent, in the process he did come to know what he was doing and with whom he was consorting. In late 1943, Domvile joined the Constitutional Research Association (CRA). His decision to join this group gives insight into his beliefs. The CRA was formed by members of the National Socialist Party that had been founded to support the idea of Nazism. Its leaders, Lord Haw-Haw, John Beckett et al. were former members of the Fascist BUF who were expelled for criticising Mosley.

Major Harry Edmonds, a former intelligence officer, was one of the leading founders of the CRA. It questioned the truth of genocide by Germany and opposed the Nuremberg trials. It led anti-Semitic opposition to the Bretton Woods agreement and opposed American power, particularly in Europe. The Bretton Woods Agreement was a major shift in the system for monetary and exchange rate management established in 1944. It was presented at the United Nations Monetary and Financial Conference held in Bretton Woods, New Hampshire, from July 1 to July 22, 1944. Under the agreement, currencies were linked to the price of gold, and the U.S. dollar was seen as a reserve currency linked to the price of gold.

Edmonds was being watched by Special Branch and they recorded a meeting he had on 12 August 1943 in a Fleet Street pub with a leading Fascist A.K. Chesterton who was a politician and journalist. He helped the establishment of right-wing organisations in Britain and opposed any break-up of the British Empire, He further argued against any further immigration to Britain. Other members of the far right were present. The meeting discussed the setting up of an organisation to 'preserve British culture against the Jewish menace'. CRA grew out of this idea.

In a meeting at the Charing Cross Hotel on 28 January 1944, an agent of MI5 was present and made a report on the whole proceedings. Those attending were Harry Edmonds, Barry Domvile, General Fuller, Captain Russell Grenfell (Ex-Navy and a Daily Telegraph reporter, he was a strong opponent of the Nuremberg trials and blamed Nazi atrocities on the Allies and anti-Nazi resistance), and Rex Tremlett (editor of the fascist paper 'The Blackshirt') among others. They were all connected with BUF and fascism. Throughout Domvile's diaries we find that Horace Rex Tremlett was an early Fascist contact of his. He continually notes seeking him out to consider events and possible action. The agent's report outlines the conversation was anti-American, anti-Jewish and all believed the British Empire was finished and therefore a united Europe including Germany was the answer. Tremlett commented that if MI5 knew of their activities 'they would all be arrested'. The agent noted that Domvile, because of his deafness, spoke little but did lament that international finance had hindered the establishment of the 'New Order' and that Jewish-backed America had bombed Europe in order to be able to lend finance for rebuilding. All present agreed with his analysis. It is likely that Domvile's association with these Fascists, who had deserted Mosley, began to cause Mosley to grow cold on Domvile politically. It is also possible at this stage that Domvile had hopes of secretly resurrecting the Link. An intercepted letter from a Mary Foss in December 1944, sees her write to thank Domvile for a calendar and being 'very proud to be welcomed as the first post war member of the Link'. She goes on to write that she hopes 'it will not be long before I can publicly [she underlines the word] claim this honour'. Foss was detained under 18b and sent to Holloway because of her pro-German views. She was honorary general secretary of Prisoners of War Assistance Society (POWAS) which was seen by the Special Branch as a cover for fascists and it only helped those who were in sympathy with their views. The records on POWAS are held at the National Archives, in London.

In 1945, the secret files of MI5 show a record of an intercepted telephone call to a newspaper, in which Mosley is asked to confirm that he is associated with Domvile in the Independent Nationalists' Party. Mosley makes it very clear that he is not associated with the group and has 'no intentions of being so'. The record reports a meeting in May 1945 between Domvile, Captain Ramsay and Norman Hay at which each 'solemnly undertook to continue the fight for National Socialism whatever the outcome of the war'. Domvile stated he admired Nazi Germany and regretted that 'the Jewish power was too strong on this occasion'. Captain Ramsay applauded the 'rise of anti-Communists in the country' and believed a 'post-war campaign against the Jewish Bolsheviks stood every chance of success'. The group also discussed the idea of Mosley as the leader of a post-war group but decided he was a 'money grabber' and an 'opportunist'.

The Security Service's files also show they were still very concerned about Domvile's activities with such groups. A note in their files for January 1946 makes this clear:

'DOMVILE though aging, remains a prominent fascist personality and is determined to devote his remaining years to a revival of National Socialism. He is in touch with many of the extreme pro-Nazis as we have learned from his H.O.W. [the order to intercept Domvile's mail and telephone calls]. We should be handicapped without it.'

These intercepted letters showed Domvile's continued support of various fascists, including Mosley, who were being attacked in the press or being investigated by the police.

Domvile was also a regular contributor to the *Patriot* over this period. The *Patriot* was a far right weekly journal that was a vehicle for fascist propaganda. As was noted earlier, Domvile used the pseudonym 'Canute' as he used in *Action* and through his son's letter and Domvile's intercepted correspondence MI5 were able to confirm that Domvile was in fact Canute. Around this time he was also actively supporting the British People's Party which was on the far right, speaking at their meetings in support of candidates. MI5 files have a secret report of one such meeting in Domvile's file that describes the anti-Jewish nature of the speech. There is also the castigation of British policy against Germany and the neglect of the Empire. The speech argues that the war was really Jewish-inspired on behalf of the world's financial system and because Jews were put into concentration camps in 1933.

The MI5 files as late as 1946 show that Mosley's mail was being read by them. Between 14 and 18 June 1946 they took note of a series of letters between Mosley and Domvile. Nothing of great import was found.

In 1948 Mosley was noted by MI5 as personally fond of the 'elderly naval officer' but regarded him as a 'grave political liability'. In referring to Domvile's detention during his appeals committee hearing, Mosley said, 'A distinguished Admiral was imprisoned with us, together with his wife, but neither of them had anything to do with this group or with our party.'

This was blatantly not true. Lady Domvile had admitted she was an active member of the party and was totally in awe of Mosley. Domvile himself was heavily involved with them in different ways. His diaries show he was a regular attender at their headquarters, a regular contributor to their paper and was present at many significant secret meeting with Mosley. Furthermore, Domvile was asked to work with Captain Pitt-Rivers 'to cleanse' the BUF – hardly a job for someone not having 'anything to do with this group or with our party'. This was simply one of many attempts by Mosley to re-write history in his memoirs.

By 1949, MI5 had recorded that 'Sir B Domvile is a personal friend of Mosley, but is politically very much against him'. This was proven to be so in Domvile's growing relationship with Arnold Leese. He tried to evade internment under 18B but eventually he was caught and detained. Released in 1944 due to failing health, he once more returned to his extreme activities which included helping German SS prisoners escape from British custody. He returned to jail on being convicted of this offence.

Domvile's intercepted letters show his support for Leese. In 1950 he writes to Leese agreeing to act as surety. 'Yes, certainly I will act as surety, provided they do not value you so highly as to make it ridiculous. I am awfully sorry they have caught you again.'

A few weeks later he writes again. 'I was sorry to see that your forecast was correct. As they have chosen to put you to this inconvenience, I hope you will lose no opportunity to make things unpleasant.' In this letter Domvile blames the Jews for Leese's arrest, suggesting the informant, a Gentile, 'must have changed his name' [From a Jewish name].

Domvile also wrote articles for *Free Briton*. This was a journal of the Britons, another extreme anti-Semitic organisation. It also advocated a strong anti-immigration policy and was founded by the same man who influenced Arnold Leese, Henry Hamilton Beamish. The Britons published pamphlets and a great deal of anti-Semitic propaganda. It used the imprint names, Judic Publishing Company and Britons Publishing Society. They were determined fascists and clearly hoped for a Fascist government for Britain. Domvile's articles followed their sympathies. In February 1950, an agent from MI5 reported on a gathering, 'Nationalist Reunion and Social', organised by the Britons Publishing Society, which Domvile attended. MI5 noted '70 persons, including 14 women attended'.

In 1954, Arthur K Chesterton, a fascist who was part of Mosley's BUF along with Domvile, formed the League of Empire Loyalists. Domvile had a great liking for Chesterton, whom he describes in his diary as 'a stalwart'. Chesterton believed that the American capitalists and the Russian Bolsheviks had formed an alliance under a Jewish conspiracy. He therefore felt it necessary to create a group who would expose and oppose it. Domvile had been growing quiet politically but was persuaded to join this enterprise. The group was a great irritant to the official Conservative Party and carried out a number of activities to embarrass and harass them along with other groups with whom they disagreed. Domvile never took part in any of these. As with most Fascist groups, personality clashes and money issues caused the demise of the group and in 1967, they joined other anti-Semitic and Fascist groups to form the National Front. Domvile was appointed onto its inaugural National Council.

Chapter 15

What Domvile's Diaries Reveal

Domvile kept a diary for most of his life, the exception being during his stay in Brixton. These diaries were given to the National Maritime Museum following his death. Reading them immediately shows that there was a great deal of self-editing in their writing. It becomes clear that a number of meetings and events that Domvile was known to have attended are excluded. There is also a lack of the 'real man' in these records as he rarely reveals his true feelings about events. However, now and again, he appears unable to help himself and the odd entry gives clues as to his true views. They also confirm his association with many of the key characters that MI5 believed he was involved with, in their reasons for wanting him detained. For the purpose of this current work, the diaries for the period 1935 to 1950 have been covered as they span the time that Domvile was politically active. His roles after 1950 were more in acting as a name and figurehead for far right and fascist groups, including the group that led to the formation of the extreme British Nationalist Party. Along with the comments already made in the text above, we do get insight into Domvile's involvement in German affairs and friendships with leading fascist and anti-Semitic figures.

In 1937, he notes with joy the joining of the Link by 'Baroness Van der Cotton' along with a number of failed meetings with 'Karlowa and Carroll'. His entries for this year also show a knowledge that people joining the Link had direct connections with BUF. In December 1937, he mentions Sir Charles Raymond Beazley becoming involved with the Birmingham branch of the Link. One other case he records in the same month is that of Eric Whittleton who, as we have seen, agreed to organise the Acton branch. These were the sort of connections that caused the Security Forces to suspect that Domvile was involved in a Fascist plot to overthrow the British government. Throughout December, Domvile's entries show him meeting Arthur Chesterton, Gordon-Canning, Peter Eckersley and Walter Hewel among others. These were all very active pro-Nazis and anti-Semites. Frequent meetings with C.E. Carroll and Professor Laurie figure regularly.

In an entry for 7 January 1938, Domvile writes 'Pothecary of B U wants to organise an area for Link in S W Suburbs', indicating again that Domvile was very aware that the Fascists were becoming involved in his organisation. On the 27th of the same month he writes of Laurie speaking at a meeting. He adds 'Lady S very pessimistic about Halifax's visit to Hitler' and reveals his anti-Semitic views, 'I suspect more Jewish wickedness' believing in a 'whispering campaign'. Domvile's egotism regularly surfaces in his diary and February 1938 sees him boasting of success at a Chatham House lecture.

From 6 to 11 February, entries show that Heinrich Hoffman visited Domvile. As already indicated, he was the supplier of German propaganda literature for distribution within the Link. He had been the recipient of letters from BUF fascists as well as Link members in respect of this propaganda material. He is noted as having 'discussed Nazi policy for hours' with Domvile who describes him as 'very nice', adding, 'They are so damned intense, these Germans.' In a second entry Carroll and Laurie are present. Hoffman is described as 'speaking in a shrill voice' that 'the Pope castrated his Vatican choir yet objected to sterilisation in Germany'. These kind of encounters suggest Domvile was well acquainted with German intentions and policies.

His diary for 22 February expresses his pleasure at Anthony Eden's resignation. This is likely because Domvile was a great supporter of Neville Chamberlain and his appeasement of Hitler and Mussolini. Eden came into conflict with Chamberlain and his policies and resigned. Eden's comments reported by Alden Whitman of the New York Times made this disagreement clear:

'It was not over protocol, Chamberlain's communicating with Mussolini without telling me. I never cared a goddamn, a tuppence about protocol. The reason for my resignation was that we had an agreement with Mussolini about the Mediterranean and Spain, which he was violating by sending troops to Spain, and Chamberlain wanted to have another agreement. I thought Mussolini should honour the first one before we negotiated for the second. I was trying to fight a delaying action for Britain, and I could not go along with Chamberlain's policy.'

Across Europe there was a background of a growing concern about Hitler in Germany. He had established concentration camps at Dachau, Sachsenhausen and Buchenwald. He had declared his policy on *Lebensraum* and expansionist plans. He had made clear his alliance with Mussolini. In England, people like Domvile were advocating a policy of non-intervention and appeasement with Hitler. His rejoicing at Eden's departure and the removal of an opponent of accommodating Hitler, demonstrates his pro-German/Nazi views.

The 4 March 1938 entry confirms that Domvile was well aware of the growing presence of fascists within the Link. He records speaking at a bookshop on it, where twenty people were present, 'mostly Fascists' and he 'got seven new members'. It was also around this time that Domvile makes notes on the intention to bring the Link into the offices of Carroll's *Anglo-German Review*. On 17 March 1938, he confirms writing to Ribbentrop. We also find him meeting up with Gordon-Canning and Mosley. He writes of attending a rally where Mosley was speaking and describes him as 'a demagogue'. He records Lady Domvile 'worked up' with the Nazi salute, but he states, 'I found this beyond me in England'. It is possible that this may suggest he would take part in this when *not* in England as was suggested during his hearings before the committee. He further calls Mosley 'a great leader' and he 'likes his policies' and 'he [Mosley] will succeed'. Fascists were regular visitors to his home and he refers to 'the local Fascist chief and her daughter' coming to lunch with his wife. The May 1938 entries confirm his relationship with Himmler being very cordial. He receives 'a long letter' from him about a Tibetan expedition. The expedition was led by Ernst Schäfer, a German zoologist and SS officer. It was described as a scientific venture but was a vehicle used by Himmler for propaganda purposes. Because there were five SS officers involved, it was suspected to have secret military objectives. There is also evidence of his being a great defender of Germany and Germans. One note describes a 'long argument' with 'two diners who hate Germans'.

Domvile was a member of the AGF and it appears regularly in his diaries. As we have already noted, the AGF was allied to *Deutsch-Englische Gesellschaft* in Germany, This German group was under the control of Ribbentrop the German foreign minister and ran parallel to his ministry. He often met with Philip Conwell-Evans, one of their leading figures.

This organisation was perceived to be Nazi leaning and continued to exist long after many similar organisations closed when Hitler came to power. Lord Mount Temple, another of AGF's leaders, made a public statement declaring that they had no sympathies for Nazism but he resigned in November 1938 as chairman of the AGF because of the treatment of the German Jews by the National Socialists.

A June 1938 diary entry confirms Domvile's opposition to Winston Churchill, when he describes a speech he had given criticising him, made to Link members. He seems to enjoy the occasion, writing, 'it went down well'. He also notes the meeting was 'packed by LNU [League of Nations Union]'. The LNU was a large organisation wanting peace in Europe and had Austen Chamberlain, brother of Neville Chamberlain on its council.

Domvile seems to have a ready route to get things to Germany through the German Embassy in London. He sends books of his own to Germany this way. He also notes in the Diary 'A Mr Hodges wants a book to be given to Hitler'. Domvile gives it to the German ambassador to pass on. In June 1938, he is also with the ambassador at a party. Domvile surprisingly notes 'there were lots of Germans there'. Is that not what you would expect at a meeting organised by the Germans?

It is at this party on 15 June he meets Ribbentrop. After the party Domvile writes to Himmler. He does not say what the correspondence was about. Two days later, Domvile is visited by Baron von Rheinbaben, an apologist for Hitler. He was a former member of the Reichstag and a diplomat. He toured Europe assuring people that Hitler had no evil intentions. In one speech in 1941, after the start of the war, he said:

'Germany knows that Europe's strength and character lie in its plurality. There is no question of eliminating it, rather, it will be a case of orientating it towards a modality of common economic and social defence: to make Europe European.'

Rheinbaben gave Domvile 'a long talk', no doubt reassuring him that Hitler had 'no evil intentions'.

Insight into Domvile's anti-Semitism surfaces in an entry on 10 July 1938. He writes about Leslie Hore-Belisha and objects to 'paying for police protection for this Jewish Don-Juan'. Hore-Belisha was appointed by Neville

Chamberlain to the post of Secretary of State for War. Throughout his career, Hore-Belisha was dogged by anti-Semitism, despite having served with distinction in the Great War, rising to rank of Major. Lieutenant-General Sir Henry Pownall wrote about him and his falling out with General Gort, the Commander-in-Chief of the British Expeditionary Force:

> 'The ultimate fact is that they could never get on – you couldn't expect two such utterly different people to do so – a great gentleman and an obscure, shallow-brained, charlatan, political Jew-boy.'

Gort had been particularly stung by criticisms made by Hore-Belisha when he visited the front during the war. Eventually, with pressure from men like Domvile, Hore-Belisha was reluctantly removed from office by Chamberlain.

In a further entry in July, Domvile was giving 'the low-down about Hore-Belisha' to 'a Fascist from headquarters'. This also reveals Domvile as a member of the BUF, referring to its headquarters as his own very frequently throughout his papers. Later that month, he dines at home with Mosley and Gordon-Canning and 'Pudd sat next her *Führer* [Mosley] – was blissfully happy'.

MI5 suspected Domvile was in a conspiracy with Mosley's fascists. An intriguing entry for 2 August 1938 points to this. Domvile has dinner with Mosley and shows him 'the correspondence between Himmler and Chamberlain'. This correspondence can only have come to Domvile from the German side and his contact with Himmler. This kind of knowledge could indeed be dangerous in Fascist hands opposing any government intending to go to war with Germany. A month later, Domvile receives a letter from Himmler but he does not reveal its contents. Later that month, Chamberlain and Hitler signed the agreement in Munich much to the delight of Domvile, 'I am so happy with Chamberlain and Hitler.' The diaries continue to give insight to those helping the Link. One such helper, Hopple, 'only became pro-German when Hitler came along'.

Domvile's further acceptance of fascists into the Link came in 1939. His diary shows that in February of that year he is in 'discussions with the Anglo-German Brotherhood [AGB]' to affiliate with the Link. They in effect cease to exist and become part of the Link. This group was composed mainly of clerics who wanted to promote links with German churches, but many of their ranks supported Fascism and were members of Mosley's BUF. They seem to have believed that the Link was a natural home for them.

Domvile frequently mentions in his diaries meetings with Germans, often making notes. On 14 February 1939, he meets two Germans with Carroll and records 'one of them knew Darlington well'. He also makes reference to receiving a letter from Hoffman in the next day's entry. On 27 February, he gives a talk to the Link, commenting in his diary, 'several Germans were there'. In the first week of March he also receives a visit from a German called Heller and '2 Danzig Germans'. Heller seems to stay for a few days. On 7 March 'a young German from Dusseldorf' arrives. He brings a plaque to present to Domvile, stating that he 'was the only one working for friendship [with Germany] in England'. On 6 April 1939, we find two German officers on leave are visitors to Domvile's home.

There is a remarkable entry on 17 April 1939. Domvile writes, 'sent a memo to Carroll of advice to Hitler, which will be forwarded to Germany' with another note 'Back to the 14 points'. We now know that this was at the time that Hitler was planning the rejection of the Germany-Poland non-aggression pact. The fourteen-point plan was that of President Woodrow Wilson, which formed the basis of the Versailles Treaty, which Domvile did not agree with. Was Domvile directly liaising with Hitler giving him advice on the Treaty and his dealing with the British Government?

Professor Laurie visits Domvile and tells him about the concentration camps reporting that 'Czech Slovak being let out after inoculation with germs of leprosy'. Domvile adds a note 'These women will believe anything'. The following day he writes of an 'Ellen', 'she wanted to incite the people of this country against Germans' and continues, 'she must be crazy'. Domvile is either living in denial of the reality or deliberately refusing to accept the situation. The newspapers were running reports of the horror of camps. The *Essex Newsman* in 1939 was typical of such reports:

'The continent of Europe is now a hell of slaughter and suffering. Czechoslovakia, a crucified nation, eight million of them going through months of horror and mental agony.'

Domvile continues to support Fascism in writing of the BUF's *Action* paper, 'it's quite splendid'. He also records sending a poem to Mosley. On 2 July

1939, Domvile attends a BUF Seminar. Later on 10 July, he is angry at the cancelling by officials of a meeting for Captain Ramsay (the Right Club). His anger is clearly directed. 'The power of these bloody Jews is alarming.' He confirms his support for the distribution of handbills for Ramsay. It is clear from a diary entry on 14 July 1939 that Domvile was in fact 'thinking of a plan to unite all the parties who think the same on foreign policy'. He also attends a cocktail party with Germans which was 'full of leaflets'. He makes no comments on the content of the leaflets.

It is over the next few weeks that Domvile records his wife's activities in which she becomes infatuated with the British People's Party (BPP), floating between them and the BUF in her affections. He seems amused and pleased with her. He supports her activities by declaring his backing to St. John Philby, the British People's Party candidate, in the Hythe by-election The British People's Party was an anti-Semitic and pro-Nazi group. They opposed any war with Germany and any interference on the European continent by Britain. This was entirely in line with Domvile's own views. They were extremely Fascist in their beliefs and principles. On 16 July 1939, he attends a grand fascist rally by the BUF in Earl's Court, 'a la Nuremberg', in his note. He comments that 'all were giving Nazi salutes'. He again demonstrates his own adoration of Mosley, 'OM [Oswald Mosley] spoke for 2 hours. Perfectly splendid.' The meeting's layout reminded him of 'Hitler's layout' at Nuremberg. On 20 July his wife joins 'the inner council of the BPP'.

Once more Domvile receives a visit from 'a nice man from Danzig' who gives him 'the news'. On 26 July, Domvile attends a 'large dinner' with Ramsay, Mosley and Professor Laurie among other fascists and pro-Germans. He also records a meeting around this time with George Ward Price, also an associate and confident of Oswald Mosley. He was a member of the BUF and a leading journalist, who Hitler had described as 'the only foreign journalist who reported him without prejudice'. Price also wrote kindly of Hitler, praising his kindness and love of children and dogs. He declared him intellectual and well read. Ward Price was also a very close associate of Domvile and was one of the first to ring him when he got his knighthood. This was noted in Domvile's diary for 3 June 1934. Regular entries throughout the diaries show contact with Ward Price. After the war and defeat of Hitler, Price would distance himself from his earlier comments.

At the end of July and early August, Domvile went to Germany. Over his visit the diary gives little insight into his activities there. We find he spends a lot of time with Olive Baker who he had regular correspondence with in England and as we have noted would later spend time in prison for pro-German activity. It was rumoured that she in fact was his mistress. Domvile's comment on her imprisonment was 'Poor little fool'. They both meet up with Hoffman, he lunches with her and sits and writes letters with her. On one occasion he describes her as 'kind Miss Baker'. He meets Goebbels and appears to be fond of him and he shares the 'Royal Box' with him. He also comments in the entries that 'Carroll's money arrangements had nearly landed'. This entry suggests that Domvile knew more about Carroll obtaining finance from Germany than he admitted at the hearings. We also discover his immediate reaction to Samuel Hoare's announcement in parliament about the Link. He calls him, 'a lying sod' and promises to 'make him pay someday'. Considerable time is spent on the telephone to English newspapers. He also meets up with Walter Hewel, Hitler's foreign affairs adviser for 'an interesting chat'. Domvile gives him a letter from a 'Miss Alport' to be given to Hitler.

On 7 August 1939, Domvile noted that 'Old Laurie left out of newspaper report for the £150 he got for his book'.

Back in England on 28 July, Domvile meets up with Newham, the editor of *Truth*. He also records that Carroll 'paid 2/6 for the Duke of Westminster's Link's fees' and considers it 'a good advert'. This is an interesting phrase as it is the same as he had used for the publicity for the pro-German NBBC. When questioned about that, he pleaded not knowing what he meant. However, he believed that the Duke joining the Link would be good to promote its cause. This suggests that Domvile's use of the same phrase for NBBC was in the same spirit, that is, promotion of the NBBC's giving the German point of view. The next day after sleeping on it, the diary notes, Carroll advised Domvile that it would be 'unfair to publicise the Duke of W joining'.

October of 1939 is an interesting month in the diary. MI5 had concerns about Domvile's involvement with various pro-German groups. He had tried to distance himself from them; however, the diaries do show he had very regular contact with them. On 7 October he meets Norman Hay of Information and Policy for a long visit and calls him a 'very able and interesting man'.

On the 17th he makes special mention of a '3 hour meeting' with Pitt-Rivers. He was his co-speaker at BUF gatherings. On the 18th he has a long meeting with Gordon-Canning of British Council for Christian Settlement. Then on the 26th he has a meeting with Professor Laurie, Captain Ramsay, Lord Tavistock, Norman Hay and Oswald Mosley with some others representing various groups. At this meeting, Domvile notes Mosley acknowledges him (Domvile) as 'the instigator of the meeting'. Four days later, he visits 'BUF Headquarters to talk to the editorial staff of *Action*'. Pitt-Rivers also appears to meet Domvile regularly.

On 8 November, the diary has an entry that describes a meeting with Norman Hay outside Oswald Mosley's house, where Domvile was going for a meeting with Mosley and Ramsay. Hay warns Domvile against Henry Drummond-Wolff. Drummond-Wolff was an anti-Semite and initially pro-Nazi. He donated money to Mosley's BUF and was active in trying to prevent war with Hitler. The Duke of Westminster was impressed with a plan he had to create a revolution in Germany to distract Hitler from war with Britain. He was thus becoming less inclined towards BUF and it was likely this that brought about Hay's warning.

The diary for 9 November shows that Domvile was friendly with Norah Elam (Dacre Fox). He has dinner with her and her husband and describes them both as 'red hot members of BUF'.

On 22 November, Domvile attends Oswald Mosley's talk on 'The menace of freedom'. He meets up with Mosley again on 6 December 1939 and takes pleasure in noting that Mosley 'congratulates' him for his articles in *Action*. There is also a meeting with Fascists and others in which Domvile joins in a drink and a 'silent toast to the leader' which 'makes the old bitches eyes round'. He does not indicate who 'the leader' is, however, this was a term used by Lady Mosley of her husband. In late December, he also confirms he is writing to *Truth* criticising Churchill. Early January 1940 sees Domvile visiting 'BUF HQ' and his entry on 30 January is strange. He writes, 'listened to Hitler'. This presumably was via the NBBC and appears to confirm his understanding the German language.

The diary has details of the meeting Domvile was invited to by Lord Tavistock regarding the Dublin peace proposals to prevent the war. A number of Fascists were present and they 'perused Hitler's peace terms from German Embassy in Dublin'. Domvile felt 'they were quite reasonable'.

The result of the meeting was that they 'settled on a policy. We must fix Chamberlain and Halifax down'. Two days later Domvile is at the BUF HQ meeting Mosley, who 'was interested in Tavistock's meeting'. The following day, *Action* printed an article from Domvile entitled, 'Britons Beware'. Domvile attends a second meeting on Tavistock's plans on 29 February.

In March 1940, Domvile introduces Olive Baker to Mosley. The entry for 13 March 1940 details a meeting with Tavistock and Mosley 'on peace talks'. When Domvile was questioned by the appeals committee, he did not mention this particular meeting. The entry ends 'L G to lead peace Government'. This can only refer to the elderly Lloyd George who, as we noted, had met Hitler in 1936.

There are a number of entries that record Domvile meeting Mosley and attending the BUF HQ. On occasions he notes that the chats were 'good'. He also has entries confirming his listening to Lord Haw-Haw on NBBC.

He did not keep a diary whilst in internment in Brixton. On his release he once again began to write his diaries. He still remains anti-Jewish with one of his first entries declaring his resentment of 'Jewish controlled media'. After his release the diaries hold little of interest as his influence wains. He remains a figurehead of a past era and useful to the new fascist blood. In the 1945 diaries he records his comments on his *Patriot* articles. He remains in contact with Carroll and other old Fascist connections. The entry for 1 May 1945 records Hitler's death being announced and Domvile's view that it was 'a better way to go than Mussolini'. In 1946, he carries out a few speaking engagements, usually around Empire matters. The 1947 diaries record his reunion with Oswald Mosley and they exchange books they have written. They also reveal that Domvile is still trying to create another form of the Link or Fascist movement along with Carroll. He is in touch with the League for European Freedom, an organisation that was anti-Communist and connected to criminal Nazis who had cooperated with America and Britain. Oswald Mosley had been approached to join this new 'Fellowship' but was 'not interested'. By now MI5 are losing interest in him but he is still feels under suspicion on one occasion writes of a café visit and claims, 'Freud's son works there as a waiter and I expect an MI5 spy.' He also notes in his diary that he 'suspects the mail is being tampered with'.

Overall, the first thing that strikes the reader about all the diaries is the mundaneness and often boring nature of the entries. Domvile delights in recording his daily walk with his dogs and his dining out. He also records the films he went to see, the theatre visits, along with comments on the happenings of a normal household. He delights in dining both out and at home and in the back of the diaries lists the books he had read in that year.

Chapter 16

Domvile in *Action*, *Patriot* and Other Writings

When Domvile retired from the Navy he wrote his memoirs, *By and Large*. In them, we do get some glimpses of his views. He called the Jews, 'the bees in the Nazi bonnet'. Domvile at this time is not totally clear in his attitudes. On one hand he complained to Himmler about anti-Jewish banners he saw outside towns and villages, yet whilst he agreed there was harsh treatment of Jews he would not adopt a 'sloppy sentimental attitudes towards the Jewish race'. He also advised that there was 'no reason for our being so intolerant with the policy of others, as well as with their methods of conducting it'. In a twisted Biblical reference, he also wrote, 'Jewish ways are not our ways, neither or their thoughts our thoughts.' In his book, he also referred to the press being so agitated by Jewish ill-treatment because the press was 'so thoroughly impregnated' by Jews. The book leaves us in no doubt that he was totally taken in by the Nazis and their system describing it as 'excellent'. What this book does show is that Domvile appears to be wrestling with an inner anti-Semitism and yet a humanitarian concern for how they were being treated in Germany.

He wrote for Fascist papers and it is noticeable that on one occasion he wrote under his own name and he is very careful about what he writes. Domvile wrote for *Action* in June 1939. The article is under his own name and emblazoned with his titles, 'Admiral Sir Barry Domvile, K.B.E., C.B., C.M.G.'. In the article, 'IT SHALL BE PEACE' the whole argument is that the British government should be making peace with Germany. If only the Government would do as he suggested and appease Germany, then it would be peace. His reason for the possible war is not the Jews or the Masons but oil, which is the closest he comes to referring to the Jews and the Middle East. Just three months before war broke out, he is here advocating that Britain should not go to war with Germany. His argument is from his long held view of Empire first. He considered Britain should ignore a Germany growing in power. He ends the article using a word that has huge weight, but not in the sense used today:

> '*And what of the end of the Holocaust?* [Original article has italics here]
> 'There will still be 80,000,000 Germans – or what is left of them – in conditions exacerbated by the recent conflict. The problem will remain, but it will become far more difficult to find a solution in the general wreckage of Europe.'

The 7 December article has Domvile suggest that Britain should have been in an alliance with Germany and France, with Germany taking the lead against Bolshevik Russia. The article is a tirade against Communism but as always, Domvile sees the Jewish conspiracy:

> 'Already there are signs that the old gang are trying to put over the same confidence trick that succeeded in 1919. It is not called The League of Nations this time but the Federated States of Europe or something of that kind. It is unnecessary to add that many of its sponsors are of Jewish origin.'

Writing as 'Canute' and believing he is under anonymity, the issue of oil is no longer mentioned. Jews have now become responsible for the war.

Furthermore, he also calls for Mosley and other fascists to be brought into the Government's council. In January 1940 the article 'Change of Heart' in *Action*, Domvile addresses Lord Halifax who had suggested that Hitler should retire into 'the obscurity for which his character fitted him'. Domvile derides Halifax and continues his theme of a change of government 'to bring immediate peace'. Once more, he declares the character of Hitler has been distorted by a 'Jewish-controlled' press. He also insists that 'Herr Hitler did not want this war'.

By February 1940 Domvile, in his guise as 'Canute', is now in a rage. Under the title, 'Britons Beware' he is in full anti-Semitic flow. He declares 'the Jews have had enough of war' and adds that "they have cleaned up nicely'. More than this, he claims Jews 'have provided some excruciatingly enjoyable methods of robbing Christians'. He also goes on to declare, 'Anti-Semitism is increasing so rapidly that the Jewish position in the land of dreams is seriously threatened.' He claims 'they [the Jews] have decided to cash in.' Then he moves into conspiracy theory by arguing that Jews have not given up 'getting their claws into Germany or of funding the Jewish World State'. Then sarcasm becomes his tool. 'We are told for world peace, sovereignty must be handed over to a central Sanhedrin [the ancient Jewish court system] – beg pardon- council.' This is followed by more conspiracy theory:

> 'Abraham, Isaac and Jacob are not specifically mentioned as the directors of the new international Paradise, but a brief study of this impudent scheme leaves no doubt. … The British Empire … is to be handed over for destruction to the evil power of Jewry.'

However, he argues that it will not succeed because there are organised countries in Europe who will fight to the death to stop it, presumably Germany being one of them. Yet he argues that there is 'a grave danger' that the 'so called democracies' will create a 'Federal Union' which he believes is 'a world surrender to Jewish finance and chicanery'. He then berates the 'titled back-sliders' who he sees as selling their heritage for 'a mess of pottage' adding 'shame on them!'. His final flourish is to decry 'the all-pervading influence of the Jew'. There can be no doubt that, free from identification, as he thought himself to be, Domvile's true views are revealed in this particular article.

It is also interesting that a review of his book *By and Large* on 23 April 1940, has the Fascist reviewer state, 'Sir Barry holds no brief for the Jews and the subject of Hebrews in Germany is treated in the manner which we expect from a Briton and not in the mawkish sentimental terms of our "uncontrolled" national press.' That was an understatement.

In the action of 7 March 1940, Domvile responded to a speech on the war by Lord Halifax. Halifax had been talking to young men who would be joining the army to fight Hitler and he had made it clear it was Hitler's fault. He had also told them that the war was their war, in that they had the opportunity to bring an end to Nazi aggression. Domvile as Canute, is in full sarcastic mode:

> 'Vanished is our belief so many of us honestly cherished that the war began when the international financiers [Jews] cracked their whips over

the team of performing seals sitting around the Cabinet table at number 10 and gave instructions for the slaughter to commence. Your pardon, Abraham! Forgive me Isaac! Let bygones be bygones Jacob! It was none of your work.'

He then then bemoans that Mosley is 'not being allowed to tell the truth'.

In the *Action* article on 21 March 1940, Domvile addresses a retired soldier, who I believe is himself. He writes of how this figure is considered a traitor because he criticises the Government's handling of the war with Germany. As a response, he joins the BUF and Domvile advises him he has no cause for feeling he is a traitor and is entitled to his pension for services rendered. Once more he derides the Government as 'performing seals' and argues again that Germany did not want the war.

His article on 4 April 1940 in *Action*, continues to use the derogatory term 'performing seals'. He refers to 'Stanley – the War Seal' and Churchill as 'the Blubber Seal'. He decries the 'daily dope from our Jewish National Press'. He then goes on to blame Oliver Cromwell for bringing the Jews back to England. This shows an ignorance of history as the banishment bill to banish the Jews was never revoked and Jewish immigrants simply re-settled in England without harassment. However, he goes on to claim that this gave the Jews 'an opportunity to establish the stronghold on our national life'. In ending he argues for a negotiated peace. In his article of 18 April 1940 he turns his sights on the government's decision to drop leaflets onto the German population. He writes:

'The Seals [British government] undoubtedly thought that when they blew their little paper trumpets on the outbreak of war, and showered their confetti on German soil, the wall of Nazidom would fall flat like the wall of Jericho in the Bible story. Whoever could have persuaded them to believe such arrant tosh?'

He is of course referring to his conspiracy theory that the Jews were behind the war. He does not believe the leaflets will have any effect and continues to deride the government for anticipating German bombing raids on England. He himself 'never for one moment anticipated air raids'. He believes the Government may not be telling the truth and, as he did before the appeals committee, recommends *Falsehood in Wartime*. He also claims Hitler was 'the man who raised them [the Germans] out of the dust'.

These excerpts from Domvile's writing can leave no doubt that he held anti-Semitic views and was certainly pro-German/Nazi. There are also strands of evidence that he did want a change of government and one that would include Mosley.

After his release, we find him again writing as Canute in another Fascist paper, *Patriot*, and still believing that he was anonymous. In a Canute article in *Patriot* in October 1946, under the banner WANTED! MORAL COURAGE, Domvile protested that British people should stand up in defence of the Nazis at Nuremberg, as, in his opinion, they were doing their duty, liking them to the suffragettes who suffered and died for their cause. It was under this pseudonym in the following month he wrote another letter to the *Patriot* about the Nazi war criminals executed at Nuremberg. He argued that 'the Nuremberg victims died bravely, and are more likely to survive in history as martyrs than criminals.' One of Mosley's branch secretaries, unaware that Canute was Domvile, wrote to the *Patriot* to say that Canute's views were the same as those of Mosley.

Continuing to demonstrate his anti-Jewish stance, Domvile, as Canute in the *Patriot*, wrote on the subject of the Balfour Declaration. This was a proposed homeland in Palestine for a new Jewish State contained in a letter from Foreign Secretary Arthur James Balfour to one of Britain's prominent Jewish citizens, Baron Lionel Walter Rothschild. Domvile derided the choice of Palestine and suggests that Zionists were behind a conspiracy to make Palestine the homeland. They were a Jewish nationalist movement that has had as its goal the creation and support of a Jewish national state, *Eretz Yisra'el* (The Land of Israel) in Palestine, the ancient homeland of the Jews. He revives his long held belief that Siberia under Stalin was the right place for Jews. He sarcastically discusses anti-Semitism and suggests Siberia should be offered and if refused then no one could ever charge anyone with anti-Semitism when discussing Jewish matters.

Domvile was not yet done with Nuremberg. In July 1948, another Canute article returned to the subject. Under the title 'NÜRNBERG THE AFTERMATH', he termed the proceedings 'unsavoury' and called them a 'travesty of justice'. Once more he returned to his favourite theme of the *Protocols* and the Jewish conspiracy theory. He argued the trials were a preparation for the 'One World Communist State ruled by Zion'. He brings into his argument the execution of Charles I, claiming it a similar case and goes on to suggest that Cromwell was pressurised into the execution by Jews from whom he wanted a loan. This is clearly another case of Domvile believing false ideas circulating in Fascist circles. There is no historical evidence for this claim and is another pointer to Domvile's anti-Semitic views. The Canute articles all follow a similar theme and invariably took an anti-government stance, criticising the leading figures of the day. It would also seem that his pro-German views were increasingly now closer to pro-Nazi views in his defence of them at Nuremberg.

By 1948, Domvile, now seventy, was growing into his old age and still convinced of a Jewish plot to take over the world. A speech he had prepared was taken by his old Fascist friend A.K. Chesterton and produced as a pamphlet. It was entitled, *The Protocols and the Push for World Government*. In it, Domvile bemoans the 'moral' decline of Britain because 'we have passed more and more the control of our international mentors'. He contrasted the current British government who he argued had 'began to flirt with the notion of a One World policy' and 'our forefathers' wise conception of Empire'. His belief was that the government had 'the misfortune to fall under alien influence'. He then makes clear who he believes is that alien influence, 'international Jewry'. Although clearly blaming the international Jewish community, he sarcastically writes, 'I am not blaming the Jews in any way.' He then proceeds to recount the damage to 'true British interests' and lays the blame on the 'domination of alien councils'. He then argues that The League of Nations was the first step to this One World and immediately links it to the *Protocols*. Whilst acknowledging that these had long been charged as forgeries, he nevertheless claims that for him 'they have never been satisfactorily disproved'. This is despite the huge evidence amassed by this time that they were indeed a fiction.

Domvile continues to outline his views on the conspiracy and attempts to defend the *Protocols*. He accuses the British politicians of having 'staked their politics on the horse from the Zionist stables' and that 'international Jewry' had made 'sweeping charges of anti-Semitism to aid their cause'. All this he insisted 'was provided for in the *Protocols*'. With claims of bribery and corruption he then sets out his concerns for workers. He storms against Communist ideas of liberty for workers as well as those of Attlee who proposed that workers should have rights and laid out his principles in *The Social Worker* in 1920 and Churchill with his ideas for social insurance and who both supported the ideas of ensuring good conditions and wages for the employed. In outlining his own views of liberty for workers, he saw it from a right wing nationalist perspective. This was in line with the ideas of Italian Fascists and Corporatism that had crept into Britain and sought a break from democratic government. Mussolini himself had said, 'Fascism should more appropriately be called Corporatism because it is a merger of state and corporate power.'

Domvile would add to his anti-Semitic pronouncements with the publication of other books, *Straight from the Jew's Mouth* and *The Truth about Anti-Semitism*. This latter book was issued with a rather provocative cover that had the usual anti-Jewish caricature swatting a starfish in the shape of a Swastika. Domvile was still marching to the drumbeat of anti-Semitism and far Right politics. He also put pen to paper to make known his views on the Freemasonry conspiracy, with the publication of *The Great Taboo: Freemasonry*.

The book he wrote during the war and published when it had ended was titled *From Admiral to Cabin Boy*. This book was his reflection on his detention and laid out his belief in the conspiracy between Jews and Masons to rule the world and cause his downfall. This belief pervaded his entire thought. For example, he wrote:

> 'After the arrival of Hitler and the impetus thereby given to German rearmament, British policy changed under the guidance of Judmas, which disliked both the German treatment of the Jews, and the German new economic doctrine which threatened the reign of Gold.'

It was not only in Germany that he believed Jews to be active because for him 'the Jews who were running and ruining the country [England]'. In this book he argued, 'In vain we pleaded that we had never attacked the Jews', yet here he was doing just that in the very same book as well as under the anonymity of Canute in *Action*. He also states the conspiracy in plain words:

> 'For the aim of these international Jews is a World state kept in subjection by the power of money, and working for its Jewish masters.'

Indeed, even Churchill was part of the plan:

> 'Churchill is one of the leading Jewish enthusiasts in the country, and the Jews are generally credited with having an undue influence in the creation of Governments. Possibly they entertained the belief that Mr. Churchill would be a suitable head-butler, provided he did not drop the tray too often, in which event he could, presumably, be ruthlessly dismissed. I do not know. No need for him to be a Mason, because he holds already the most advanced views on Internationalism, and must be a source of daily delight to the Learned Elders: a Rabbi's rapture.'

These allegation, innuendoes, claims and views of and about Jews appear throughout the book. Domvile had left no doubts about his opinions on the subject of the Jews and his anti-Semitic credentials, this despite his denials.

Conclusion

MI5 files had amassed a great deal of evidence on Domvile. He had clear links to *The British Council of Christian Settlement* and the *January Club*. The letters from Domvile to Luttman-Johnson and his own diaries reveal he had regular meetings with him, often having lunch at the Cavalry Club in London. The government were certain that there was German influence and control of the Link, despite Domvile's assertions that the original idea of the Link was innocent. There was no doubt that the Ribbentrop Bureau had supported the Link through Carroll. Then there were the reports sent to Germany being made by an unnamed Nazi leader in Birmingham on Link meetings. Carroll also reported to the Ribbentrop Bureau that, 'the Link remained steady throughout the crisis' and that some of their members were resigning from the Territorial Army, refusing to fight against Germany.

There was clear distribution of German material at Link meetings and many pro-Germans and supporters of the Nazis had been given a platform. Whilst it could be argued that the evidence that Domvile had close links with the Nazi leaders is thin, there is no doubt he had been very welcomed in Germany and was close to Himmler. He also hosted many Germans at his home before the war and revelled in their attention. His attendance at the rallies in Germany was admitted but many prominent members of the aristocracy from Britain had also attended. It would be impossible for Domvile to deny an association with Ramsay and the Right Club. It clearly had a connection with the Link. The curious claims by Domvile not to have known the contents of Laurie's book are also suspect. Through his diaries and meetings were it was discussed, he at least must have had an inkling as to what Laurie was promoting.

The abundance of evidence that is available leaves no room for doubt that Domvile had close contact with the far right. Many of his friends and colleagues were members of Mosley's BUF, the Right Club, the January Club and other similar groups. His association and closeness with people like Olive Baker, Luttman-Johnson and Maule Ramsay cannot be ignored. The common link he had with these people was anti-Semitism, pro-German leanings and an admiration of Hitler and his strong grip on Germany and its people. Indeed his defence of German attitudes was evident in his speeches:

'They nearly all seemed to impute the desire for war to other countries, principally Germany and Italy. It was a curious manifestation that peace loving nations should be accused of a desire for slaughter and blood lust.'

In the same speech on the subject of Jews and expressions of condemnation of Germany's treatment of Jews, he said:

'Whilst the persecution of the Jews, or any persecution for that matter, created feelings in this country, we certainly would not help the Jews by a campaign of vituperation [against Germany]; but we can only ameliorate their condition through the influence of our friendship with Germany.'

Domvile would reject the label 'Fascist', however, there is clear evidence that he not only embraced the principles of fascism but was involved in its organisation. His friendship with Mosley was more than simple dining and pleasure. His articles in Action and the Patriot demonstrated beyond doubt where his sympathies lay. Furthermore, like Mosley, Domvile's writings and actions were clearly in favour of Germany and he never welcomed Britain's involvement in war against her. He remained 'bitterly opposed to the war' calling it 'a folly'.

These matters, alongside Lady Domvile's activities as a member and supporter of the BUF that were listed, provided the basis of the case against Domvile. After the hearing and perusal of the material, Domvile was informed in December 1940 that he would be remaining in Brixton Prison. He felt it 'unsatisfactory' that he was not told the committee's verdict or the reasons for his further detention, blaming it on 'Judmas' in his book *From Admiral to cabin Boy*.

To come to any conclusion about the questions surrounding Admiral Sir Barry Domvile, we have to take account of the climate in which he lived.

The history of Germany has been fraught with military invasion and war. The First World War and the Versailles Treaty left a bad taste in the mouths of Germans. People like Domvile and other military men, who had fought against Germany, also felt that the victors, especially the French, had been unfair to Germany, This is one element that spurred him to seek better relations with Germany.

Secondly, he also felt that he had to protect the Empire and did not want any involvement with the continent of Europe. His view was that peace in Europe should be left to France, Italy, Germany and Russia to sort out. He was an old fashioned military man who held that there should be honour among former enemies and that reconciliation was important. His pro-German views are therefore understandable in that context.

However, there are questions raised that Domvile never seemed to answer. These were the Nürnberg Blood Laws and the subsequent treatment of Jews and other minorities. Why had he never fully condemned them without reservation? The reports from Germany were quite prolific and clear. The majority in Britain were convinced of their veracity. It was a minority, usually on the far Right and of Fascist leanings, who argued otherwise. His continual defence of the Nazi regime suggests that he had moved from being pro-German to being pro-Nazi. Many in Britain who had been pro-German abandoned their stance once the direction of travel by the Nazis became clear – Domvile did not.

When we look at the issue of anti-Semitism and Domvile, we have to again understand the times he lived in and the history of Britain and the Jews. The Jewish people throughout their history have been persecuted in almost every country in which they lived. There are, of course, myriad reasons for this, most of them stemming from before the advent of Jesus Christ. In the ancient world, because of their strict adherence to their faith of monotheism, along with their food and cleansing laws, they stood out in a world of polytheism.

Since the advent of Christ, their religion suffered more persecution as charges of being the 'the Christ killers' added to the many other slanders against them. Even though these charges and claims have been exposed as ignorant and fallacious and rejected by the majority of those who have made intelligent enquiry, there has remained a deep seated, and often unconscious, anti-Semitism. In Germany, the matter was further complicated by the religious revolutionary beliefs of Martin Luther. He had moved from attempts to convert Jews to his beliefs and when they refused he became a virulent anti-Semite. His writing, although it has to be seen in the context of the rough language of the time, is still chilling:

> 'First to set fire to their synagogues or schools and to bury and cover with dirt whatever will not burn, so that no man will ever again see a stone or cinder of them ... Second, I advise that their houses also be razed and destroyed. For they pursue in them the same aims as in their synagogues ... Third, I advise that all their prayer books and Talmudic writings, in which such idolatry, lies, cursing and blasphemy are taught, be taken from them ... Fourth, I advise that their rabbis be forbidden to teach henceforth on pain of loss of life and limb ... Fifth, I advise that safe-conduct on the highways be abolished completely for the Jews ... Seventh, I commend putting a flail, an axe, a hoe, a spade, a distaff, or a spindle into the hands of young, strong Jews and Jewesses and letting them earn their bread in the sweat of their brow, as was imposed on the children of Adam ... But what will happen even if we do burn down the Jews' synagogues and forbid them publicly to praise God, to pray, to teach, to utter God's name? They will still keep doing it in secret. If we know that they are doing this in secret, it is the same as if they were doing it publicly ... for our knowledge of their secret doings and our toleration of them implies that they are not secret after all and thus our conscience is encumbered with it before God.'

It can be clearly seen how his views influenced many Nazis and why they were picked up as their excuse for their programs of extermination. Alongside this the forgery of the *Protocols* gained traction and fuelled the Nazi hatred of the Jewish people.

The majority of Christianity has now rejected the views of Luther on this matter, but in Domvile's time there were still many within the Church who still held to anti-Semitism and a sizeable minority were found in the ranks of Fascists and groups such as the Anglo-German Brotherhood.

We also need to understand that in Britain, there was a history of the rejection of Jews and indeed they had been expelled in their entirety from England in 1290, by King Edward I. Some did remain and practised their religion in secret. Under Cromwell they began to return, even though Edward I's statute was never revoked. Even before this, in 1275, Edward I passed the law *Statutum de Judaismo*. This absolutely forbade Jews to lend on usury, but granted them permission to engage in commerce and handicrafts, and even to take farms for a period not exceeding ten years. Furthermore, if a Jew did become a Christian, his conversion was considered a larceny of the Lord, and his property and goods were confiscated. There was also a rule that they were not allowed to appear in public without some badge or mark of distinction. The Nazis were not the first to apply this. Later, Edward relaxed the usury rules a little but they had been excluded from many of the normal occupations and were forced into a few professions, one of which was an underground system of finance and money lending. Because of the Jewish religious restrictions on usury, only Gentiles could be charged interest and with Edward's statute they resorted to extorted bonds that included both principal and interest. The Jewish people were forced by Edward into poverty and to exist they had to resort to what was by the strict wording of the law, illegal. This became a point of anger and jealousy in the Gentile communities and led to further resentment. Shakespeare took this up in his play, *The Merchant of Venice*.

As a consequence, in 1278 the whole English Jewry was imprisoned and no less than 293 Jews were executed at London. It is incredible to think that the rule on a Jew being identified in public by an article of clothing was not revoked in England until 1846. It was the early 1800s before the Jews were given respite from legal restraints on their ability to earn a living. This background echoed down the ages and became an ingrained seam that ran down every royal line and throughout the aristocracy. However, it is also true that it weakened in its intensity down the ages and not everyone in the Royal household held onto the prejudice of Edward I.

However, we also have to note that the Royal Household in England were descended from German stock. Whilst they did not bring with them any desire to persecute the Jews or treat them in any way as the Nazis did, they did have what has been described as 'mild anti-Semitism' and as we have shown above, with Edward VIII it remained.

Domvile was a Royalist and was a member of the upper echelons of society who shared the anti-Semitism described above in various degrees. However, it does appear that he would be included in the stronger end of that spectrum. He was well-read. His diaries include details of the history books he read. His knowledge of this history, including that of the Jews, though sometimes flawed, would have allowed him to look at the Nazi treatment of Jews as no different from times past. He would therefore consider it none of his business. As long as it was happening in Germany, then for him, as he had said and written, it was the concern for the Germans and not the concern of Britain.

It is with these understandings we can now turn to look at some conclusions about each of the charges that caused Domvile's detention.

I. *Founder and stable of the Link.*

This claim against Domvile is beyond dispute. He was the main mover in the Link's founding. He had travelled up and down the country promoting it and there is no doubt that without him the organisation would have collapsed. His money and time were necessary and his service reputation and titles essential for its promotion.

II. *Was closely associated with prominent Nazi leaders in Germany and in this country.*

The association with Nazi leaders could hardly be called 'close'. There is no doubt that he had met them and indeed showed some admiration for them. He was also well known to Himmler who had shown great hospitality to him in Germany. There was correspondence between them and a measure of friendliness in the exchange of greeting cards. With Goebbels, there does seem to have been some relationship that was more than brief. Letters had been exchanged between them and he had accorded some measure of importance to Domvile in Germany with the invitation to review troops. Domvile denied any ability in speaking German using that to deflect any closeness to the Nazi leadership. However it is clear that he did have a grasp of German. Why would he deny this?

III. *Is sympathetic to Germany and the Nazi system of Government.*

This flows from the previous charge. As was indicated above it is always necessary to set Domvile against his times and his worldview. Domvile was a passionate believer in the British Empire under the rule of the British royal family. He believed in a world conspiracy of Masons and Jews taking control of the whole world order. He also believed that Bolsheviks were a major threat inspired and directed by what he termed 'Judmas'. Therefore, after the First World War ended, Domvile wanted the British government to focus on the Empire and leave Germany to look after itself.

When the Versailles Treaty was drawn up, Domvile, quite rightly, saw that it could never be swallowed by Germany and that eventually it would erupt in trouble. He therefore was sympathetic to Hitler's claims that the Treaty was not good for Germany and should be able to take back the colonies. Domvile appears in his writings to agree with this. Furthermore, when it came to the large German-speaking population in Czechoslovakia, Domvile also sympathised with Germany looking after 'their own people'. There was also the Jewish issue in Germany and Hitler's treatment of them. Domvile again did not make any major complaint about it, simply saying it was the result of 'the revolutionary processes' involved in Germany taking steps to secure its future. His anti-Semitic views led him to an indifference to their treatment, continually leaving it as a matter for Germans.

He also had written a foreword to *The Case for Germany* which itself was not only sympathetic to Germany but lauded her and her Nazi leader Hitler. His denial of the content of the book stretches credulity. Domvile was extremely well read and when it came to matters about Germany he was keen to keep up to date with events. There is also a note in his diary that this was one of the books he had read. Furthermore, he was present at the book's launch and heard Laurie talk about it. So again we are led to question his truthfulness in this matter.

We also know from his writings under the name Canute that he regularly praised the Nazi system and its policies. We also know that he attacked Churchill for his condemnation of Nazi atrocities and did his best to support understanding of what the Nazis had deliberately done to innocent people caught up in the war. Through secret meeting and open speeches and writing Domvile did everything he could to support the appeasement of Hitler. It is certain that he authored the letter to *The Times* in London supporting the Munich Agreement.

Finally, Domvile was also convinced that France was a weak country and could not be trusted to deal with the Communist threat from Russia. He therefore was supportive of the idea that Germany should be encouraged to be the frontline against Communist expansion and that Britain should ally with her and support her efforts. For these reasons, the claim that Domvile was sympathetic to Germany and the Nazi system of Government appear to be well founded.

IV. *Has been closely associated with Sir Oswald Mosley and other prominent leaders of the BUF.*
This charge cannot be disputed. Domvile's diaries show regular meetings, both open and secret, with Mosley. He was a regular dining companion and Domvile worked with him often. He recorded in his diaries showing him the Tavistock peace proposals for Germany and meeting to discuss how they could be advanced. We know Domvile attended Mosley's public meetings and his diary shows him attending private lectures. There are recorded meetings between Domvile, Mosley and other Fascist leaders including Pitt-Rivers, Ramsay and Beamish among others. Then we have the whole business of Mosley's BUF paper *Action*, to which Domvile contributed regularly as Canute. Both men were very aware of the authorities being concerned about their activities and thus they tried to play down their relationship. Despite all denials, it is certain that Domvile was in fact a closet member of the BUF and that his wife was not only a member of the BUF but closely involved in its inner circle.

V. *Has been active in the furtherance of the objects of the BUF.*
With what was written above about Domvile's association with Mosley, it follows that Domvile was happy to support the objects of the BUF. This was mainly in respect of its policies on the British Empire which were to defend and further its interests around the world. That Domvile was closely supportive of furthering the objects of the BUF was clearly seen in the secret meeting to agree a 'purity campaign' that he would lead with another fascist, Captain Pitt-Rivers. This was a campaign to ensure that the objects of the BUF were not harmed by the wrong elements being admitted to the

organisation. Furthermore, his writings in *Action* as Canute were designed to promote views which were central to the BUF.

VI. *Has since the outbreak of war discussed with Sir Oswald Mosley and other prominent members of the BUF the coordination of Fascist activities and the achievement of Fascist revolution in this country.*

Domvile made a great play about closing down the Link on the outbreak of the war in 1939, with the king's enemies being his enemies. However, this did not prevent him continuing to meet with Mosley, Pitt-Rivers, Gordon-Canning and others to 'discuss the progress of the war'. The king was never a problem for Domvile; it was always the government he had problems with. Again, background is important. Oswald Mosley had long tried to get to power through the Conservative and Labour Parties. He even had tried to organise his own Party to achieve this. All these avenues failed and he became an isolated figure from the mainstream of politics. As a Fascist, Mosley believed in the idea of Corporatist government and the abandonment of traditional democracy. The strong hand of leadership by Mussolini and Hitler was attractive as a style suited to ensure the implementation of this form of Government.

We know from Domvile's writing that he also liked the idea of Corporatist government as he outlined in *The Protocols and the Push for World Government*. Once again, Domvile was outlining the conspiracy of the 'One World Order'. He saw this as a threat to the Empire. Arguing that 'The Government was committed to a policy whose details it was not prepared to communicate to the public,' he also derided the idea of Trade Unions as Communist-inspired and went on to describe what he felt was best for the workers; this was the idea of 'National Guilds'. This was allied to the control of industry by its Guild workers with the ideas of 'Social Credit' and would flow through all parts of society including schools. These ideas are similar ideas to those underlining Hitler's arguments in National Socialism and the 25-point Programme of the Nazis. Hitler himself had also argued against Communism and Capitalism. Indeed, Hitler and the Nazis believed in the medieval corporatist society and that a Germanic tribal society of peasants should serve as paradigms for the Third Reich. The whole idea of Corporatism is seen in these views and Domvile's rant against Government is also seen in the final passage of the document:

'The former [his ideas] is LIBERTY. The latter [government ideas] is capitalistic regimentation of the worst order, and Englishmen will never lie down behind an iron curtain and allow their Crippses, Attlees and Churchills to spout deceptive words about liberty and prosperity while hammering on the shackles of nationalised slavery in a carefully calculated level of rationed poverty for us all.'

Therefore, Mosley and Domvile would be ideal bedfellows for each other in their ideas for an alternative Government; both would have welcomed a form of Anglicised Fascist rule under royalty in Britain. We saw from Domvile's comments about the return of Edward VIII as a sign of this. Indeed, Mosley's own words after his arrest are clear. 'I will continue to do my best to provide people with the possibility of an alternative government.' Domvile had also allowed Whittleton to take over the Acton branch, and Whittleton had argued for a move from democracy to a government that would oppose Jewry. In his Canute articles in *Action*, Domvile continually attacked the Government and even suggested that Mosley and other Fascists should be brought into the government's council.

In this last point is how a 'Fascist Revolution' in this country would have been a possibility. Hitler had been agitating for years against the elected German government, just as Mosley had done against the British government. Eventually, Hitler was invited to join the German government to bring peace to the country. This is probably what Mosley had always wanted for Britain and had failed to do through the normal political channels. We know that many secret meeting had been held with Domvile, Mosley, Ramsay, Pitt-Rivers and other Fascist leaders in the country. There is no doubt from what has been written by these people and by what MI5 discovered through agents that they indeed would have welcomed a change of government. Their government would have immediately sought peace with Germany and allowed Hitler to pursue his own plans, whilst they pursued the idea of Empire. The question was always how they would bring about their schemes and the evidence suggests that it would be by infiltration of

Government rather than violence. It would appear that this was the substance of the secret meetings that Domvile attended.

Guilty or Not Guilty?

With all this in mind we can turn to the detention of Domvile and consider whether it was a step that had to be taken. Before that however, the whole idea of detention of anyone without trial and due process has to be looked at as a matter of principal. When the regulation came to parliament there was considerable concern about detention without trial. On 31 October 1939, Mr Dingle Foot spoke for many MPs in the House:

> 'I come now to the detention of suspects. Nobody can dispute that in these regulations the suspect may be imprisoned without trial for an indefinite time. It is true that there is an advisory committee before whom he can state his objections, but I do not think any hon. Member, certainly no hon. or right hon. Member from the Treasury Bench, will say that that is a proper substitute for trial in a court of law.'

Sir J Anderson in the same debate stated:

> 'The Regulation 18B is designed to enable the Secretary of State to take action which is essential in the public interest in regard to persons who are not technically enemy aliens. There are many such persons, British subjects, who are entirely alien in sentiment and are British subjects only by reason of a technicality.'

Whilst in a time of war the government was able to detain enemy aliens, British subjects were always immune from such threat. Now the government felt it right that even British subjects who showed sympathy with an enemy should come under the same scope. There were attempts to get the government to seek a judge's order to endorse such detentions but this was defeated. In the end, despite all opposition the Regulations were passed. The concern was for the safety of the Realm and to ensure that those considered as a threat to the country in war time could be removed from circulation and any possibility of supporting the enemy avoided. So in this wider view, many were considered a danger and thus detained. However, because there was no judicial review, it is true that many were incarcerated who should never have been detained and who would never have harmed their country. Therefore, if there is a view that any detention of a citizen of a country without due legal process is wrong, then Domvile should never have been detained.

However, with the detention legislation in place, we can look at the more specific case of Domvile and the decision to detain him. There is no doubt that Domvile held pro-Nazi, anti-Semitic, and Fascist views. It is also clear that he would have welcomed a change of government that would make peace with Germany. There is no evidence that suggests he would have involved himself in a violent overthrow of authority, but rather would look to a peaceful transition.

Furthermore, would the former admiral who had served his country assist the enemy in time of war? MI5's view was that Domvile was a 'bit of a fool, who liked a drink and had mistresses'. They believed he liked the kudos of his title and rank and wanted to be seen to be important. They also considered whilst Domvile would not aid a German invasion, if one occurred and was successful he might possibly become involved in a post-invasion administration. This has credibility, if the Nazis would maintain the idea of the restoration of the Duke of Windsor. Having reviewed the documents and material relating to Domvile, one gets the impression that this old admiral would be happy to be involved in a bloodless and very British coup, one in which the king was in charge of an Empire and with a country that was free of foreign influences, particularly Jewish. A country that did not have the inconvenience of democracy but was governed by Corporatism were both capitalism and unions were tightly controlled – a country where everyone knew their station in life. Ultimately it could be deduced from the Secret Service records and the many comments that Domvile in himself was not a problem, but that it was the use others might make of him that was the issue.

It does appear that often he would be deceived by those around him, like Carroll and his admiration for Mosley which blinded him to that man's manipulation. From all evidence it appears that whilst he had contact with Germans and he may have felt important, they in turn do not seem to have held him in any great significance; that was also the conclusion of MI5. One does get the impression of a man who held the prejudices of his peers around him at the time, and who let his concern for the Empire blind him to everything else. There is no doubt that he did go down the route of friendship with Germany as an ideal, but allowed himself to be hijacked by people with a totally different agenda. As matters progressed, he appears to have more and more been consumed with the idea of conspiracy and allowed his own prejudices to develop and for them to be encouraged by men like Carroll, Mosley and Ramsay.

Domvile unfortunately appeared naïve in his dealings with these more dangerous men who would have delighted in either of them being the Emperor in Domvile's Empire. Domvile was seduced by the Nazi and Fascist propaganda. Goebbels himself said, 'The essence of propaganda consists in winning people over to an idea so sincerely, so vitally, that in the end they succumb to it utterly and can never again escape from it.'

This is indeed what appears to have happened to Domvile. None of this excuses Domvile from taking responsibility for his actions, but in the end he was a dangerous and deluded old fool, who for his own sake, the authorities believed needed to be given a berth in Brixton.

Even though he continued after the war to be involved in far Right politics, it was always as a name, and the detention without trial was his badge of merit and passport into the hearts of the extremists of the far Right. In the end, there is no doubt that Domvile's views are repugnant to any decent civilised mind and should be challenged and rejected but it is unlikely he would have done anything deliberately to harm his country. Indeed, Domvile, the Munich Man, asked the question, 'I wonder what our descendants a hundred years hence will have to say about it?' referring to the Munich Agreement. What Hitler said of those that made the agreement is telling. 'I saw my enemies in Munich, and they are worms.' Surely, therefore, the answer to Domvile's question is written by the blood of the 85 million worldwide who died in the Second World War and those whose bodies went up in the smoke of Auschwitz and the other death camps of Europe. There is no doubt in most military minds that the appeasement of Hitler allowed him to develop his strategies and a stronger response right from the beginning would have changed history. Even Neville Chamberlain eventually noted, 'It is perfectly evident surely now that force is the only argument Germany understands.' Indeed, MI5 had sent a report to Chamberlain saying that he should 'not delay for a minute to prepare … for a total war' which unfortunately he ignored.

We turn to Domvile's friend Goebbels to show us the how Domvile was fooled into joining with those in Britain who espoused Nazism and Fascism and wanted their own dictatorial government:

'We enter parliament in order to supply ourselves, in the arsenal of democracy, with its own weapons. If democracy is so stupid as to give us free tickets and salaries for this bear's work – that is its affair. We do not come as friends, nor even as neutrals. We come as enemies. As the wolf bursts into the flock, so we come.'

Bibliography and Sources

Resources consulted

Griffiths, Richard, *Travellers of the Right*, Oxford University Press, 1983.

Lockhart, Sir Robert Bruce, *The Diaries of Sir Robert Bruce Lockhart, Volume 1*, Macmillan, 1973.

Luther, Martin, *The Jews & Their Lies*, 1543 Christian Nationalist Crusade 1948 ed.

Reid Gannon, Franklin, *The British Press and Germany*, Clarendon Press, 1971.

Sutton, Claud, *Farewell to Rousseau*, Christophers, 1936.

Tennant, E W D, *True Account*, Max Parish, 1957.

Zámečník, Stanislav, *That Was Dachau*, Le Cherche Midi, 2004.

Ziegler, Philip, *King Edward V111*, Collins, 1990.

Periodicals and Newspapers

Whitman, Alden, *Career Built on Style and Dash Ended with Invasion of Egypt*, *Anthony Eden's Obituary*, New York Times, January 15 1977.

Graves, Philip, 'The Truth about the Protocols: A Literary Forgery', August 16–18, The Times of London, 1921.

Arnold-Foster, W, *Germany's Concentration Camps: Nineteenth Century and After*, Leonard Scott Pub. Co, 1933.

Rheinsbaben, Baron von, *Vers Une Europe Nouvelle,* Presented at a lecture in Maison de la Chimie in Paris, 1941.

Archives

MI5 Files Barry Domvile, Captain Maule Ramsay, Oswald Mosley, National Archives, London.

British Newspapers Archive 1935–1946.

British Union of Fascists Newspaper, *Action* 1930–1945.

The *Patriot* Newspaper, 1920–1945.

The Age Newspaper.

Records of the January Club.

Hansard 1930–1945.

The Diaries of Admiral Sir Barry Domvile 1934–1960, courtesy of the Caird Library at The National Maritime Museum, Greenwich, London whose staff were ever helpful and efficient.

Index

Abrahams, Marc, 60
Abyssinia, 15, 58
Ackworth, Captain Bernard, 46
Action Newspaper, 16, 30, 57, 78, 93, 108, 114, 122, 125-6, 128-9, 131, 133-5, 137, 143-5, 151
Aikin-Sneath, Brian, 83, 84
Albania, 48
Allen, Mary Sophie, 56, 57
Allen, Lord, 73
Alsace-Lorraine, 4
Anderson, Sir J, 146
Arnold, Lord, 46,
Arnold-Forster, William, 12, 150
Auschwitz, 148

Baker, Olive, 39, 52, 56, 90, 97, 106, 124, 126, 137
Baldwin, Stanley, 16, 65, 131
Balfour, Arthur James, 64, 132
Bassett-Lowke W J, 34
Beamish, Admiral Tufton, xiv, 103-105, 116, 143
Beaufort, Admiral Sir Francis, 23
Beazley, Professor Raymond, 34, 35, 46, 117
Beckett, John, 112
Bedaux, Charles, 17, 18
Bedford, Duke of, 55, 56, 85, 110
Bernstorff, Count Albrecht, 58
Birkett, Norman, 28, 71-4, 77, 78, 80, 82-8, 90, 92-101
Bismarck, Otto Von, 2, 31
Blackshirts, 29, 30, 107, 113
Blanchard, Edward, 83
Bolsheviks, 13, 17, 114, 116, 129, 142
Bothamley, Margaret, 35
Boyle, Nina, 56
Braunau-on-the-Inn, 1, 2
British Council for Christian Settlement in Europe, 39, 41, 52, 55, 77, 85-6, 100, 125, 136

Brock, Sir Osmond, 24
Brocket, Lord, 31
Brown, Sir John, 34
Buchenwald, 20, 119

Carroll, Cola Ernest, 21, 34, 37-8, 44-52, 74, 76, 81, 84-6, 88-9, 91, 94-5, 97-8, 101, 109, 112, 117-19, 122, 124, 126, 136, 147-8
Chamberlain, Austen, 120
Chamberlain, Houston Stewart, x
Chamberlain, Neville, 18-19, 21-2, 25, 34, 45-6, 70, 98, 118, 120-1, 126, 148
Chesterton, A. K., 113, 116-17, 133
Churchill, Winston, 11, 54, 56, 64- 5, 69-70, 78, 95-8, 120, 125, 131, 134-5, 142, 145
Churchill, G. P., 71
Clark, Sir George, 97-9
Collinson, Professor W E, 71, 80
Conwell-Evans, Philip, 14, 119
Corporatism, 22, 134, 144-5, 147
Cotton, Baroness Van der, 117
Crawford, Archibald, 34
Crooke, Sir. John Smedley, 46
Curzon, Cynthia, 29, 30
Curzon, Lord, 29
Czechoslovakia, 4, 19, 20, 45-7, 52, 122, 142

Dachau, 20, 27, 66-7, 75-6, 109, 119, 150
Dacre-Fox, Nora, 39, 78-9,125
Darlington, Lord, 122
Dawson, Lord, 14
Dawson, Geoffrey, 31
Dawson W. H., 46
Drummond-Wolff, Henry, 51-2, 125
Duke of Wellington (5th), *see* Wellesley, Arthur Charles

Eckersley, Peter, 117
Eden, Anthony, 16, 118-19, 150

Index

Edmonds, Major Harry, 112-3
Edward VIII, 17-8, 27, 58, 140, 145, 147, 150
Eicke, Theodor, 66
Elam, Nora, *see* Dacre-Fox, Nora

Fairfax, Lord, 46
Ferdinand, Archduke Franz, 2
Forster, Dr Edmund, 6
Foss, Mary, 113

Galloway, Lord, 31
Godfrey, Admiral, 97-8
Goebbels, Joseph, 18, 20-1, 30, 35, 37, 41, 58, 72, 124, 141, 148-9
Goering, Hermann, 13-14, 18, 73, 89
Gordon-Canning, Robert, 38, 51-2, 85, 100, 112, 117, 119, 121, 125, 144
Gort, John Vereker, 6th Viscount, 121
Gowlland, Colonel Edward, 57, 91
Grenfell, Captain Russell, 113
Gutmann, Hugo, 6

Halifax, Lord, 118, 126, 129-30
Hardinge, Viscount, 46
Harker, Oswald Allen, 84
Haw-Haw, Lord, *see* Joyce, William
Hay, Norman, 51, 54, 79, 109, 114, 124, 125
Hazlerigg. Sir Arthur, 71, 80, 86
Healey, Cahir, 62
Henderson, Sir Neville, 18-19
Hess, Rudolf, 13, 18, 72, 89
Hetzler, Dr Erich, 44, 47, 90
Hewel, Walter, 37, 117, 124
Heydrich, Reinhard, 20
Heydt, Alexandrine von de, 24
Himmler, Heinrich, 18, 41-3, 45, 50, 53, 66, 72, 75, 80, 82, 89, 112, 119-21, 128, 136, 141
Hoare, Sir Samuel, 15, 36, 48, 74, 80, 82, 94, 98, 106, 124
Hoffman, Heinrich, 100, 118, 122, 124
Holmes, Valentine, 102
Hore-Belisha, Leslie, 65, 120-1
Howard, Peter, 25
Hutchinson, Lt. Col. Graham Seton, xiv

Information and Policy Group, 38, 41, 51-2, 77, 83, 86, 90, 124

January Club, 25, 34, 38, 136, 151
Jarvis, F. C.. 46
Jerrold, Douglas, 46
Jones, Thomas, 14
Joyce, William, 27, 31, 60, 106, 112, 126
Judmas, 60, 64-70, 110-11, 134, 137, 142

Kahr, Gustav Von, 7
Karlowa, Otto Georg Gustav, 41, 44, 74, 117
Kent, Tyler, 27, 32, 65

Lane-Fox, Captain, 46
Latchmere House, 59, 62, 91
Laurie, Professor A. P., 32-7, 41, 45, 46, 49-50, 58, 77, 91-3, 108, 118, 122-5, 136, 142
Leese, Arnold, xiii, 115, 116
Lewington, H. E., 13
Liddell, Guy, xiv, 12, 17, 37, 39, 55
Lloyd George, David, xi, 4, 14, 16, 86, 126
Lockhart, Bruce, 58, 150
Londonderry, Lord, 14, 31, 42, 46
Ludivici, Anthony, x
Luttman-Johnson, Henry, 38, 51, 52, 85, 86, 100, 136, 137

MacDonald, Ramsay, 13
Maddocks, Hubert, 34
Manders, Sir Geofrey, 36
Marhau, Karl, 44, 89
Marigliano, Col. Francesco, the Duke del Monte, 27
McGovern, John, 111
Meissner, Otto, 14
Morris, John, 102, 105, 108, 109
Morrison, Herbert, 69, 103, 104, 111
Mosley, Sir Oswald, xiii, xiv, xv, 16, 21, 27-30, 32, 34, 37-40, 42-3, 47, 51-4, 56, 78-81, 84, 86, 87, 90-1, 95, 100, 107-10, 112-16, 119, 121-3, 125-6, 129, 131-2, 136-7, 143-5, 147-8, 150
Mottistone, Lord, 14
Mowbray, Lord & Lady, 73
Mussolini, Benito, 29, 33, 58, 118-19, 126, 134, 144

New British Broadcasting Company, 27, 124-6

Newham, Henry, 52, 100, 124
Nicholson, Wilmot, 46
Noakes, Sidney H., 83-92, 98, 106, 107
Nuffield, Lord, 31

Outhwaite, Alison, 49

Palm 1, 2
Patriot (newspaper), 35, 63, 114, 126, 128, 131-3, 135, 137, 151
Peel, Sir Robert, 24
Petrie, Sir Charles, xiii
Philby, Harry St John Bridger, 123
Pilcher, Gonne *St* Clair, 42, 82-4
Pitt-Rivers, George Henry Lane-Fox, 46, 56, 57, 100, 115, 125, 143-5
Price, Ward, 123

Quisling, Vidkun 27

Ramsay, Captain Archibald Henry Maule, 21, 27, 31-2, 35, 37, 46, 51, 54, 56-7, 65, 77-9, 84, 90, 101, 106, 112, 114, 23, 125, 136-7, 143, 145, 148, 150
Redesdale, Lord, 19, 31, 34, 46, 107
Rennell, Lord, 31
Rheinbaben, Baron von, 120
Ribbentrop, Joachim von, 13-17, 31, 33, 44, 88, 94, 119-20, 136
Right Club, x, 25, 31-2, 35, 38, 51, 56, 78, 90, 123, 136
Rogers, Captain Arthur, 46
Rogiste, Max von, 45
Rohm, Ernst, 66
Rothschild, Baron Lionel Walter, 132
Russell, Lord, 39, 113
Ryder, Sir Alfred Phillipps, 23

Sachsenhausen, 20, 119
Sager, Walter de, 72, 75, 80
Sax Coburg and Gotha, Duke of, 16
Saroléa, Professor Charles, 47
Schäfer, Ernst, 119
Schmidt, Paul Otto, 14

Schneppenburg, General Baron Geyr von, 14
Scholtz-Klink, Gertrud, 31
Shanks, George, xi
Seisser, Hans Ritter, 7
Sempill, Lord, 14, 34
Simpson. Wallace, 27
Snowden, Lady Ethel, 73
Solly-Flood, Arthur, 46
Stamp, Edward Blanchard, 83
Stanhope, Lord, 81, 95, 97-8
Swinton, Lord, 84
Sylvester, A. J., 14

Tavistock, Lord, 54-5, 77, 79, 86, 125-6, 143
Temple, Lord Mount, 21, 120
Tremlett, Rex, 113
Tyrwhitt, Admiral Sir Reginald, 24

Unwin, Captain Edward, 34

Versailles Treaty of, 3, 12, 15, 19, 47, 64-5, 74, 122, 138, 142
Victoria, Queen, 16, 34

Ward, Sir Albert Lambert, 34
Webster, Nesta, 46, 75
Weiss, Ernst, 6
Wellesley, Arthur Charles, 31, 39
Whinfield, Peter, 39
Whinfield, Colonel H. G., 39
Whinfirled, Muriel, 42, 43, 84
Whitman, Alden, 118, 150
Whittleton, Eric, 35, 117, 145
Wilhelm I, 2
Wilson, Bernard, 46
Wilson, Sir Arnold, 67
Wilson, Woodrow, 4, 122
Windsor, Duke of, *see* Edward VIII
Wolkoff, Anna, 27

Yeats-Brown, Francis, 25

Zámečník, Stanislav, 67